To Giulia Maria Crespi
Founder of FAI
(1923–2020)

Hidden Italy

Unveiling Art, Nature and Cultural Heritage

Hidden Italy

Unveiling Art, Nature and Cultural Heritage

SKIRA

Enriching this edition of *The FAI Book* are the numerous new properties – including historic buildings and tracts of land – that Giorgio Armani has generously decided to donate in memory of his great friendship with Giulia Maria Crespi.

An organisation such as FAI (The National Trust for Italy) "is" the set of assets that it possesses, and the perceptible growth of FAI over recent years is evident not only in the numbers of members and of visitors, which are both continuing to rise sharply, but above all in the increase in the number of properties it owns and has restored and opened up to the public. The relationship here is that the rise in member and visitor numbers – and, naturally, donations and bequests – enables the increase in the number of properties. It is a virtuous process that works both ways: new properties restored and opened to the public generate positive feedback, which can be measured by the growth in members and donations. New members and donations thus allow FAI to accept as gifts or bequests other "pieces" of Italy, and with them come the associated costs for restoration, management and personnel to cover all of the aspects involved. FAI is perennially running to stand still… more properties require more members who share the mission, and more members make it possible to take on new challenges in terms of acquisitions and restorations.

While wrestling with this wonderful catch-22, FAI continues to grow, for the benefit both of the most beautiful country in the world and of all those who identify with its history and its priceless, multifaceted beauty.

Marco Magnifico
President of FAI

Castello di Avio, Sabbionara d'Avio (Trento)

On the previous page, Villa dei Vescovi, Luvigliano di Torreglia (Padova)

GIORGIO ARMANI

FAI is grateful to Giorgio Armani
who has always supported the Foundation
and who decided to donate this volume
in memory of Giulia Maria Crespi

I had the good fortune to get to know Giulia Maria Crespi and to work with her on some high-profile projects. Forever polite, open and deeply engaged with reality, there was something about her energy that always fascinated me. I felt that way because she succeeded in transmitting all of her tangible passion for whatever it was that she was doing, and her input was always marked out by that assured Milanese touch. It was the FAI adventure that brought us together, embodying our shared desire to widen horizons and enhance the present while imagining the future.

Our first business meeting, so to speak, concerned the restoration of the Benedictine Abbey of San Fruttuoso, in Liguria, and its entire surrounding village. It was 1983, and FAI's intervention allowed me to grasp the profound meaning and great secret of that organisation, based on hoping that Italy's art and beauty are recognised and conserved, and working to make that dream a reality. To this day, FAI continues to toil incessantly, thanks to the example set day in, day out, by its unforgettable president, who was at the helm for 34 years, from its inception up until 2009, during which time she displayed great self-sacrifice and tireless commitment. Over the years, I learned to think of FAI as a sort of agreement amongst friends, as a meeting point for people who share projects and passions, who together – each to the best of their abilities – help to make it all possible. If we all take part, though, the burden is soon lightened. We shall continue to admire and draw inspiration from the numerous marvels that belong to Italy, as we are encouraged to do by this book, which is dedicated to Giulia Maria Crespi and her work. She certainly played her part in keeping alive the dream of an unmistakably Italian sense of beauty.

Giorgio Armani

Since 1975, FAI – Fondo per l'Ambiente Italiano ETS, The National Trust for Italy, restores and takes care of special places in Italy so that present and future generations from all over the world may enjoy a priceless legacy.

FAI – **Fondo per l'Ambiente Italiano ETS**, with the contribution of everyone:

TAKES CARE
of special places in Italy for present and future generations.

PROMOTES
education, appreciation, awareness and enjoyment of Italy's environment, landscape, and historical and artistic heritage.

MONITORS
the protection of Italy's natural and cultural assets, in the spirit of Article 9 of the Italian Constitution.

Founded on 28 April 1975 by Giulia Maria Crespi, Renato Bazzoni, Alberto Predieri and Franco Russoli, FAI – Fondo per l'Ambiente Italiano ETS (The National Trust for Italy, a third-sector body) is a not-for-profit foundation that works to safeguard Italy's history, art and nature, and draws its inspiration from the National Trust organisations in the UK.

Its mission involves caring for a plethora of special places embodying Italy's cultural heritage, which consist for the most part of properties – today numbering 71, of which 54 are open to the public – that it either owns outright, through donations or bequests, or manages on a concessionary basis on behalf of individuals or public-sector bodies. The second cornerstone of its mission concerns educating people on how to learn about and engage with the cultural heritage, since this is increasingly the driver of the desire – as the right and duty of each citizen, starting with young people and students – to get hands-on in taking care of this legacy, either directly or through those, like FAI, that operate in this field in the general interest, on the basis of the principle of subsidiarity, as stated in Article 118 of the Italian Constitution. The third cornerstone of its mission is to monitor the country's heritage, supporting the State's safeguarding operations and working in partnership with the relevant institutions.

FAI was brought into being in order to "save" places worthy of being conserved for present and future generations. This approach sees conservation as a tool, leveraged to allow the properties to be opened up to the public and to enable engagement with them, so that they go from being abandoned, unknown and neglected places to places that are experienced and recognised for the value they have to offer and, as such, are protected and looked after.

For FAI, conserving is a pro-active – and, at times, transformative – process, which connotes projects targeted at restoration and change of use, as well as a programme of ongoing maintenance. Conserving is all about reinstating the historic and traditional nature of the places in question, revitalising their beauty and significance, but at the same time making them accessible, comprehensible and useable by an ever-increasing number of people, so that they may find in them an opportunity for enrichment, growth and wellbeing, both individual and collective; as such, alongside the recovery of the original purposes, they take on new functions, of service to the public, culture and recreation, while also contributing to the economic sustainability of the running of the sites. For FAI, restoration, management and cultural exploitation are operations that are complementary, integrated and all equally necessary: underpinning every project, however, is the cultural value of the places themselves, on the basis of which they are acquired as Properties by FAI, and duly restored and run.

To this end, FAI conserves the walls, works of art and landscapes, and focuses very much on preserving the spirit of the places, the authentic and special identity in which their value lies in terms of the past, present and future. That spirit is safeguarded and reflected both in the masterpieces and in the minor artefacts, and also in the stories large and small waiting to be told, which constitute an intangible heritage that is equally priceless and worth protecting, and which is fed by constant research, working in collaboration with the most authoritative universities and research bodies, and is transmitted to the public through tools that are trailblazing, effective and attractive, and clearly geared towards storytelling.

Alongside caring for and managing the places, FAI educates, raises awareness and participates in the national debate on the major issues of the environment, the countryside and the cultural heritage. The Italian landscape is under serious threat – particularly in rural areas, on mountainsides and in the villages of the inland areas – from abandonment caused by depopulation, from lifestyles and production methods that are environmentally unsustainable, and from the effects of the environmental crisis, which are becoming increasingly evident, devastating, unpredictable and damaging for mankind as well as for the environment. FAI works to benefit the environment, which is embedded in its name (*Fondo per l'Ambiente Italiano* literally means "Italian Fund for the Environment") and in its mission, and is interpreted as everything that surrounds us: the inextricable intertwining of nature and history as embodied by the landscape, representing the collective labour of generations past and present, of which we are all, therefore, at the forefront and for which we are all responsible. As such, through a strategic programme of ecological transition, FAI puts its weight behind high-profile actions and small-scale good practices with a view to mitigating the environmental crisis and adapting to its effects, starting from tangible actions in the Properties that it manages.

The network of delegations makes an extraordinary, highly effective impact on the effort to disseminate and embed the values and mission of FAI. Made up of thousands of volunteers active across all of Italy's regions, the delegations take responsibility with great commitment, determination, skill and creativity for local and national initiatives that emphasise the virtues of local areas even where there are no FAI Properties, and involve their local communities, raising awareness and mobilising citizens and institutions.

The most well-known nationwide initiatives include the *FAI Days*, in their spring and autumn editions and in the version reserved for schools. This is the largest national celebration of Italy's cultural heritage, which every year allows hundreds of thousands of citizens to discover and visit, over the course of a weekend, special places of historical, artistic and natural interest – marvels hidden in every corner of the country. In addition, the project named *Italian Places I Love,* the largest voluntary survey of cultural heritage in Italy, enables citizens to flag up places they love, which they deem worthy of protection, conservation, attention and recognition, and on which FAI succeeds in orchestrating restoration and enhancement operations that in many cases have changed their destiny, thanks also to the input of institutions and associations roused into action by the survey.

This book offers an overview of the Properties, which are at the heart of FAI's activities. They fully encapsulate FAI's mission, vision, principles and style, and above all they demonstrate the impact of its work, which each of us can see up-close by visiting them. The hope is that, after an enjoyable visit, people will want to become FAI members: in other words, to become a part of this story, so that we can all write the next chapter together.

FAI Properties

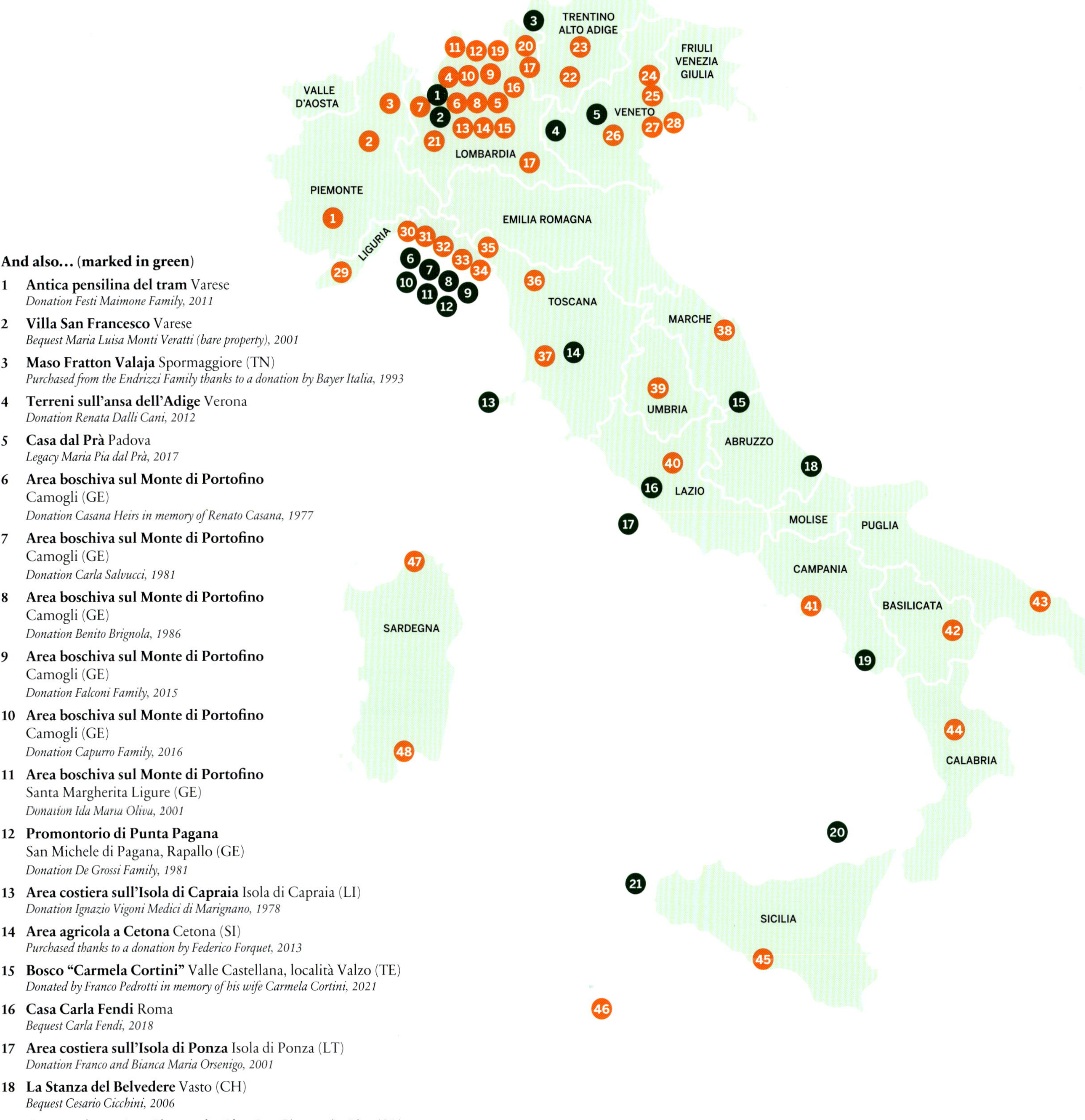

And also… (marked in green)

1 **Antica pensilina del tram** Varese
Donation Festi Maimone Family, 2011

2 **Villa San Francesco** Varese
Bequest Maria Luisa Monti Veratti (bare property), 2001

3 **Maso Fratton Valaja** Spormaggiore (TN)
Purchased from the Endrizzi Family thanks to a donation by Bayer Italia, 1993

4 **Terreni sull'ansa dell'Adige** Verona
Donation Renata Dalli Cani, 2012

5 **Casa dal Prà** Padova
Legacy Maria Pia dal Prà, 2017

6 **Area boschiva sul Monte di Portofino**
Camogli (GE)
Donation Casana Heirs in memory of Renato Casana, 1977

7 **Area boschiva sul Monte di Portofino**
Camogli (GE)
Donation Carla Salvucci, 1981

8 **Area boschiva sul Monte di Portofino**
Camogli (GE)
Donation Benito Brignola, 1986

9 **Area boschiva sul Monte di Portofino**
Camogli (GE)
Donation Falconi Family, 2015

10 **Area boschiva sul Monte di Portofino**
Camogli (GE)
Donation Capurro Family, 2016

11 **Area boschiva sul Monte di Portofino**
Santa Margherita Ligure (GE)
Donation Ida Maria Oliva, 2001

12 **Promontorio di Punta Pagana**
San Michele di Pagana, Rapallo (GE)
Donation De Grossi Family, 1981

13 **Area costiera sull'Isola di Capraia** Isola di Capraia (LI)
Donation Ignazio Vigoni Medici di Marignano, 1978

14 **Area agricola a Cetona** Cetona (SI)
Purchased thanks to a donation by Federico Forquet, 2013

15 **Bosco "Carmela Cortini"** Valle Castellana, località Valzo (TE)
Donated by Franco Pedrotti in memory of his wife Carmela Cortini, 2021

16 **Casa Carla Fendi** Roma
Bequest Carla Fendi, 2018

17 **Area costiera sull'Isola di Ponza** Isola di Ponza (LT)
Donation Franco and Bianca Maria Orsenigo, 2001

18 **La Stanza del Belvedere** Vasto (CH)
Bequest Cesario Cicchini, 2006

19 **Area costiera a San Giovanni a Piro** San Giovanni a Piro (SA)
Donation Fiamma Petrilli Pintacuda, 1984

20 **Area costiera a Cala Junco** Isola di Panarea,
Arcipelago delle Eolie (ME)
Donation Piero di Blasi, 1976

21 **Area collinare sull'Isola di Levanzo** Isola di Levanzo
Arcipelago delle Egadi (TP)
Donation Griseldis Fleming, 2001

www.fondoambiente.it

Castello della Manta

and Chiesa di Santa Maria al Castello

Manta, Cuneo

Castello della Manta
Donation Elisabetta De Rege Provana, 1985

Chiesa di Santa Maria al Castello
Commodatum from the Municipality of Manta, 1986

MANTA
SALVTIARVM MARCH:
OPPIDVM

There were many considerations which induced us, after much reflection, to donate Manta Castle to FAI. The two most important of these were to ensure the necessary maintenance and safeguarding of the Castle and its frescoes, which are of the greatest artistic value, while making these accessible to the public and – as in the case of National Trust properties in England – to keep the right to live in part of the Castle for ourselves and our heirs and descendants.

By donating it to FAI, we believe we have done the very best thing for the protection and future preservation of the Castle we love so much.

Elisabetta De Rege Provana

Elisabetta De Rege Provana.

leit
leit

The *Castello della Manta* (La Manta Castle) is located in the mediaeval village of the same name, just a few miles from Saluzzo, in the province of Cuneo, set against the backdrop of the Cottian Alps and its highest peak, Monviso. For four centuries, from the fifteenth onwards, it was the home of the Saluzzo, Counts of La Manta and Verzuolo. Subsequently, it experienced a period of abandonment, and during the Napoleonic occupation it served as a military hospital. Acquired and restored by the Radicati, Counts of Marmorito, in the second half of the nineteenth century, it was inherited by Countess Elisabetta De Rege Provana (1914–2007), who donated it to FAI in 1985, retaining the right to live in a part of the building.

On the hill of La Manta, in what was then the Marquisate of Saluzzo, a fortified complex complete with a watchtower is documented as far back as 1227. In 1416, upon the death of Marquis Tommaso III, the mediaeval fortress was inherited by Count Valerano, who was his illegitimate son but was chosen as the legitimate ruler, and who transformed it into a richly adorned noble residence.

The frescoes in the Baronial Hall, which he commissioned, are among the most important secular decorative cycles of the late-Gothic period in Europe. The paintings cover the walls in their entirety, and offer an effective summation-in-images of chivalric culture, with its myths, ideals and codes of conduct. The anonymous artist is known as the "Master of La Manta", and the painted subjects and scenes, in homage to Tommaso III, refer to the chivalric romance *Le chevalier errant*, which he wrote at the end of the fourteenth century. Resplendent on the fireplace is the heraldic motto of Valerano, *LEIT*, which perhaps derives from the German *leiden*, an exhortation to "lead", as ruler, the marquisate of Saluzzo, or according to a recent interpretation, "suffer", in the sense of coping with difficulties and hardships to reach the destination. On one side of the long walls, there is a parade of nine Heroes and nine Heroines from classical antiquity, who embody the chivalric ideals of the military and moral virtues, and where Hector, from whom the series begins, is represented with Valerano's features; on the other side, there are scenes of life, including the leisure pursuits of hunting and love, and the legendary Fountain of Youth, from which the elderly and the infirm emerge miraculously healed. The pictorial narrative is intense and vibrant, detailed and highly coloured, with scrolls that contain the dialogues between the characters and insertions of gilded stucco and metal leaves that illuminate certain details.

From 1601 onwards, the marquisate of Saluzzo, initially bound to France, was annexed to the Duchy of Savoy. Around 1563, an heir of Valerano, Marquis Michele Antonio Saluzzo, added to the mediaeval core a new apartment with a second hall, known as the "Hall of the Grotesques", frescoed in the style in vogue at the Turinese court; the Gallery is a veritable homage to Duke Victor Amadeus I of Savoy (1587–1637) and his consort Christine of France (1606–1663). The room, altered during the nineteenth century with the infilling of the windows overlooking the courtyard, was once again bathed in light thanks to a careful restoration undertaken by FAI in 2019. Other restorations have revealed the trees painted in the fifteenth century on the walls of one of the rooms in the mediaeval section of the building.

With its austere bulk, the Castle looms over the *borgo*: on the understated facade embellished by creeping vines, a large door affords access from the panoramic garden to the courtyard, where the service spaces – the Main Kitchen, the Cellars and the Wine-Fermentation Room – were also located, and from where the main staircase leads to the *piano nobile*. Since the fifteenth century, the little church at the foot of the Castle, consecrated to the Virgin, has been part of the complex. Owned by the Municipality of Manta but entrusted to FAI, its apse retains intact a second extraordinary cycle of frescoes, representing the Passion of Christ and commissioned by Valerano in 1427, in which the figures – with their heightened expressivity – recall the innovations of the Turinese painter Giacomo Jaquerio, who was one of the most authoritative exponents of the late Gothic in Piedmont.

Castello e Parco di Masino

Caravino, Torino

Purchased from Luigi Valperga di Masino
thanks to a donation by Giulia Maria Crespi
and a donation by FIAT, Cassa di Risparmio di Torino,
Maglificio-calzificio torinese, 1988

When Marchioness Vittoria Valperga di Masino Leumann died in 1987, who together with her husband Cesare had managed the castle with courage, a steady hand and generosity, hosting during the war numerous needy families, her only son, Count Luigi Valperga di Masino, realised that it would be very difficult for him to ensure the colossal family property – a veritable palace – a future worthy of its past; he therefore decided to sell the castle complete with the furnishings (over five thousand objects), the admirable historical library (25,000 volumes) and the vast family archive (which even includes a rare document signed by King Arduin of Ivrea dated around 1003–1005) to a buyer capable of guaranteeing the integrity of this formidable landscape, monumental and historical context. Count Valperga, had he wished to get the most out of the sale, could have alienated, piece by piece, the extraordinary collections of furniture, paintings, books and carriages (at the time not bound by the Superintendency) and then sell the property, but nobly put the integral preservation of the castle and the memory of his illustrious family before money; the sum requested was two and a half billion lira, less than the value of the furnishings alone. It was however a very high figure for the young foundation and if it had not been for the insistence of the lawyer Agnelli, Luigi Valperga's school friend, with FAI president Giulia Maria Crespi the proposal would perhaps not have been considered by the FAI Board of Directors. It can be said therefore that Masino Castle was donated to FAI by Giulia Maria Crespi. She never wanted it to be said, but facts are facts.

The castle, park and furnishings (some of which had come to Masino from the Valperga palace in Via Alfieri in Turin, from the castle of Borgomasino and the famous villa Pliniana on Lake Como, all of which had been family properties that had previously been sold) were, however, in an extremely poor condition and the purchase was decided only after Professor Enrico Filippi, as president of the Cassa di Risparmio di Torino, and lawyer Agnelli on behalf of FIAT committed themselves, along with Mrs Crespi, to provide the indispensable funds for the first restoration (around another 2 billion lire); the Maglificio-calzificio torinese also made a significant contribution.

Had we known – but fortunately no one imagined – that the complex in thirty years would have swallowed over 17 million euro in renovations, perhaps in that distant 1988 the die would not have been cast; but the recklessness of the young FAI led by Renato Bazzoni, the generosity and stubbornness of Giulia Maria Crespi and the support of so many Piedmontese friends, among them in the forefront Renzo and Emanuela Vallarino Gancia, ensured that today the castle, its park (restored thanks to the taste and wisdom of Paolo Pejrone) and its more than fifty rooms can look serenely to the future.

I can never forget the first time Bazzoni and I entered Masino; Luigi Valperga had already left the castle and everything was shrouded in the silence of lifeless places; the halls were dark and like two children we went from room to room, opening our eyes wide to see and our mouths wide in amazement. In the billiard room I bumped into the magnificent eighteenth-century cue holder which, devoured by generations of woodworms, fell to pieces in a cloud of sawdust leaving on the floor, along with its pieces – later to be reassembled – the skeletons of a few bats that had ended their days behind its elegant silhouette. However, the future was about to begin again: one of the longest, most complex and exciting adventures of my life at FAI.

The *Castello di Masino* (Masino Castle) is located in the Canavese area, and specifically in Caravino, a small village forty miles from Turin, which was developed at the foot of the Castle, its main road flanked by houses. Today it is home to a population of just over fifty.

The Castle sits on high ground that is part of the morainal amphitheatre of Ivrea, one of the largest and best-preserved geological phenomena of glacial origin in Europe. It was formed between 1,8 million and 10,000 years ago, when the Balteo glacier – having extended out from the Aosta Valley – began to withdraw. A document from 1070 contains the earliest reference to a fortified stronghold, over which the Castle was then built, belonging then and for more than the next nine centuries to the family of the Valperga, Counts of Masino, who could boast of a lineage stretching back to Arduin of Ivrea, King of Italy in 1002, whose remains are conserved here in the Chapel of San Carlo.

Having lost its defensive function, the ancient mediaeval structure – towers, walls, bastions and central keep – was transformed in the seventeenth and eighteenth centuries into a noble residence for the sojourns of the Masino family, with extensive grounds and showpiece halls suitable for hosting the Savoy court, with whom Carlo Francesco I (1650–1715), one of the most influential members of the Valperga family, and his descendants, including a Viceroy, Carlo Francesco II (1727–1811), were closely associated. The family occupied the Castle until 1987, with the Marchioness Vittoria Leumann (1901–1987) and her son Luigi Valperga (1930–2002) spending their summers there; in 1988, Luigi decided to sell the property to FAI, which immediately started work on a major restoration programme – the most challenging in FAI's history – in preparation for its opening to the public.

The Castle was originally accessed via what was known as the "road of twenty-two turns", due to the number of bends as it rises. This ambitious engineering project was funded by the Valperga in the 1840s. On reaching the summit, the Grande Allea leads to the Castle. This 350-metre-long boulevard is delineated by two rows of lime trees, beyond which the eye can take in the crown of the Alps and the plain of Ivrea. To one side of the Allea there is a semi-circular maze measuring more than a kilometre in length, with a thousand hornbeam trees pruned in the form of hedging; one of the largest mazes in Italy, it was reconstructed by FAI in 2009 on the basis of the eighteenth-century plans, retained along with thousands of drawings and documents in the Valperga historical archive held in the Castle.

The gradual transformation of Masino Castle from a defensive structure to a residence of leisure, intended for holidays and relaxation, also applied to its grounds, which are formed over various levels. To this day, harmony reigns between the parts of the formal Italian- and French-style garden designed in the eighteenth century – such as the Rose Garden, the Cypress Garden and the Grande Allea – and the large areas conceived in a more English, Romantic style commissioned by Carlo Francesco III (1788–1845) and his consort Eufrasia Solaro di Villanova (1789–1849). Extensive clearings – including Eufrasia's Lawn – and paths framed by high-trunked trees and flowering bushes create unexpected views, leading to the little neo-Gothic Temple designed by the Turinese architect Gaetano Bertolotti in 1826.

Arranged along the perimeter of the building is a series of terraces, some panoramic: from the semi-circular Belvedere, which is aligned with the entrance gate and offers the most wide-ranging and spectacular view, to the Lemon Tree Terrace beyond the entrance, a sort of lawned courtyard, in the corner of which, on the Castle's ancient bastions, there rises the Tower of the Winds – named for its function as a wind-powered clock – all the way to the Oleander Terrace, decorated by ten painted sundials and delimited by a second original tower, transformed inside into a frescoed round parlour.

The Hall of the Coats of Arms, which is today the first room that welcomes the public, in the eighteenth century already offered a summary image of the history and prestige of the Valperga family with the heraldic symbols of their lineage and illustrious relatives frescoed on the ceiling.

On the ground floor of the Castle there is a series of other reception rooms and private apartments. Formal banquets were held in the Hall of the Gods, which owes its name to the frescoes on the walls, depicting the divinities of Olympus. The room is enriched by furnishings sourced from Lombardy, which reached Masino through inheritances, such as the two side tables that belonged to the heroine of the movement for Italian unification, Cristina Trivulzio di Belgioioso (1808–1871) – commemorated in a room specifically set aside by FAI – whose only grand-daughter, Cristina Trotti Bentivoglio (1861–1918), married Count Luigi Valperga (1855–1935) in 1885.

On this same floor, by 1792 Count Carlo Francesco II, Viceroy of Sardinia from 1780 to 1783, had commissioned his own apartment, composed of private rooms – Cabinet of Prints, Bedroom and *Boudoir* – and reception rooms: the Room of the Three Windows, the Billiard Room, the Hall of the *Gobelins* and the Round Hall. The ancient route began from the "anterooms", which were public spaces: the Room of the Three Windows is richly frescoed with sphinxes, amphorae and coral, in dialogue with the neoclassical furniture decorated with *pastiglia di riso*, a technique using a white paste made using rice starch, which at Masino reached levels of exceptional quality. From here, the next stop was the Billiard Room and the Hall of the *Gobelins*, the latter incorporated into the apartment to serve as an anteroom, and renovated in the eighteenth century while retaining the frescoes dating from the previous century. The *chaise-longue* with gilded wooden inlays came from the famous Villa Pliniana on Lake Como, and has been in the Masino collection since the last century, as part of the Trotti Bentivoglio inheritance. The final public room was the Ballroom, created within the tower of the ancient fortified stronghold. In the late seventeenth century, it was equipped with a Venetian-style marble-chip floor and with furniture specially produced to make the most of its curved shape.

There then followed the more private rooms: the Cabinet of Prints – a little "treasure trove" with walls adorned by seventy or so prints, intended for study, conversation and the exhibition of precious artefacts – the Bedroom and the *Boudoir*, a small sitting room/dressing room adjacent to Carlo Francesco II's bedroom and used for study and personal care.

The ground floor also houses the Queen's Apartment, so-called because in the early eighteenth century Anne Marie d'Orléans (1669–1728) stayed there for a considerable time. It comprises an Anteroom, the Tower Room and a Bedroom, with seventeenth-century frescoes on the ceiling, while the walls were covered in 1780 by rice-paper wallpaper made in China. The imperial bed, with large canopy, retains its valuable eighteenth-century *chiné* silk fabric made in Lyon.

Towards the end of the seventeenth century, Carlo Francesco I put his weight behind the creation of a ceremonial route leading from the Monumental Staircase to the *piano nobile*, via the "Gallery of the Poets", culminating in the Hall of the Savoy and proceeding through the "Ambassadors' Rooms".

The route leading to this symbolic fulcrum today also takes in the Library of the Monumental Staircase, which retains the Valpergas' impressive collection of books, numbering more than 25,000 volumes, including manuscripts, incunabula, first editions, prints and drawings – a wealth of material looked after and showcased by FAI. Most of the books are stored here in the Library of the Monumental Staircase, the first inventory of which dates back to 1769 and was compiled by the polymath Tommaso Valperga, Abbot of Caluso (1737–1815). He and his brother – Count Carlo Francesco II (1727–1811) – substantially increased the number of books in the collection.

Tommaso was also responsible for the idea of the Gallery of the Poets as we know it today, which modernised the seventeenth-century decoration of the monumental corridor leading to the Hall of the Savoy by adding a series of twenty-two painted "light and dark medallions" representing the great exponents of Italian poetry, accompanied by celebratory epigrams, in accordance with a canon set by Tommaso himself.
At the end of the Gallery of the Poets, we come to the Hall of the Savoy, the heart of the *piano nobile*, sited within the oldest part of the Castle, the mediaeval keep. The frescoes that cover the walls were commissioned by Carlo Francesco I as an homage to the Savoy dynasty, their prestigious matrimonial alliances and their domains, starting from the ceiling, where a large fresco celebrates the marriage of Victor Amadeus II of Savoy and Anne Marie d'Orléans (1684) through the union of the heraldic blazons of the two houses, surrounded by standards decorated with their symbols.

A complex restoration process, undertaken by FAI in 2019 and presented to the public three years later, has made it possible to reinstate the imposing cycle of frescoes, datable to the years immediately after 1684 and in an excellent state of conservation, which emerged following the removal of the layer of white paint with which the walls had been covered in the nineteenth century. Within faux architecture, we can now once again see the views of twenty-two cities of the Savoyard territories, split between Piedmont and Savoy. On the upper part of the walls and on the ceiling, 147 heraldic coats of arms allude to the matrimonial unions of the Savoy with the main European houses of the time.
In the nineteenth century, a picture gallery was installed containing a hundred or so portraits of members of the European courts. Particularly striking for their size and importance are those of a number of members of the House of Savoy, in addition to a series of ovals with so-called "Beautiful Ladies" deriving from the renowned series of female portraits of the same name created by the painter Jacob Ferdinand Voet (1639–1689)

for the Chigi family of Rome, which were so highly appreciated as to be replicated, with variations, in the main Italian and European courts.
The ceremonial route continued in the rooms "of the Ambassadors" of Spain, Austria and France, cited in the ancient documents as the Room of Spain, the Room of the Empire and the Room of France. These rooms were frescoed with the genealogies of the respective ruling houses and furnished with richly adorned beds and furniture, embodying the purposes of hosting high-profile guests and of holding meetings, in accordance with the ceremonial court rules.

Over its long history, Masino Castle was also the administrative centre of a fertile territory, which the Valperga dynasty always managed efficiently through farms given over to the cultivation of cereals, wine and olive oil, and which today is the heart of an entire area – the Canavese – that is ripe for rediscovery, in part through the work to emphasise its virtues being carried out by FAI.
Viticulture has been practised at Masino since the sixteenth century, while from the end of the seventeenth the archival documents chart the transformation of the property from a military fortress to the preferred residence of the fiefdom. A number of rooms that had belonged to the early fortified settlements were then turned into storage rooms and cellars, and today can be visited by descending to the basement floors. The olive press would process all of the olives harvested within the fiefdom of Masino, whereas in the Cellars – an extensive space of around 700 square metres – the grapes would be vinified and the resultant wines aged and stored.
A number of farming operations are still practised today: in the area of around one hectare on the south-western slope of the estate, where the mild climate offers favourable conditions, FAI has reinstated a historic vineyard on the basis of ancient maps, planting out shoots of the typical Canavese variety of the Nebbiolo grape. The work is managed by a local winery.

Collezione Enrico a Villa Flecchia

Magnano, Biella

Donation
Piero and Franca Enrico
2011

Built between 1955 and 1970, Villa Flecchia Pirol presents itself to visitors with its simple lines and in a spectacular location. Inside, in addition to the furnishings, the Villa houses a valuable collection of paintings, fruit of the passion of architect Piero Enrico for artists who, by predilection or by birth, were part of the Piedmontese painting scene between the end of the nineteenth century and the middle of the twentieth century. Browsing through the canvases, different styles can be recognised, ranging from the beautiful romantic landscapes by Antonio Fontanesi, a nineteenth-century painter from Reggio Emilia who was very active in Piedmont, to the abstract compositions of Luigi Spazzapan from Friuli. The different artistic paths of these painters, including Matteo Oliviero, Alberto Pasini, Lorenzo Delleani, Francesco Menzio and others, find at Villa Flecchia a point of contact in the common passion for the landscape. The paintings seem almost to compete in beauty with the extraordinary panorama that can be admired from every window of the Villa, leaving the eye free to wander through the flat areas, where lush wooded areas and cultivated fields allow glimpses of small villages and then get lost in the horizon, interrupted only by the mountainous reliefs of the Serra Morenica of Ivrea. In 2011, Mr and Mrs Enrico wanted to donate the Villa to FAI with the intention, as the words of Piero Enrico himself suggest, "to preserve over time what I collected with love and sacrifice throughout my life".

Casa Macchi

Morazzone, Varese

Bequest
Maria Luisa Macchi
2015

The square of Morazzone in a vintage photo

We knew next to nothing about the intentions of Maria Luisa Macchi, an idiosyncratic, refined and wealthy lady – known in her hometown of Morazzone, in the province of Varese, as "*la Signorina*" –, until that day in 2015 on which we received her will, wherein we discovered that she had bequeathed to FAI, together with a substantial cash sum, the family home right next to the noble parish church in the town square.

An initial reconnaissance mission carried out on Google Maps offered up little of any interest, and I went to see the house in person more out of responsibility than out of conviction. I was bowled over by it. Despite still being in good health, Maria Luisa had been living for more than 40 years in a luxurious care home in Varese. She would regularly visit the small, romantic garden filled with palm, sweet olive and bamboo trees, which was also home to agapanthus plants and a majestic Japanese magnolia. However, since the time when her parents had died in the 1950s, she had not once gone into the house. Although the intact interior dated from the nineteenth century, it was like entering the only house in Pompeii that had been spared the fury of Vesuvius – indeed, every detail evoked a life that had been interrupted all of a sudden, as if due to an unexpected event. Everything had been frozen in time since that day 60 years earlier, when the doors of the house – built and furnished by Maria Luisa's grandparents and subject over time to only very few modifications – had been closed, seemingly forever, on the day of the last funeral.

Quilted satin eiderdowns (at one time, red) obscured beautiful lace covers on the numerous beds throughout the house, onto which, in the meantime, chunks of ceiling painted with strings of meadow flowers had come to "rest". In the bathroom, the long-fringed damask linen hand towels – previously pure white but now the colour of tobacco thanks to decades of dust – where still placed over the turned-wood rail, the boiler above it as immense as a submarine. Hanging in the wardrobes were narrow-waisted '50s floral dresses with three-quarter sleeve jackets, and in the dining room, on the large table surrounded by monumental chairs, duly devoured by legions of woodworms, there was a precious oriental wool tablecloth featuring a cashmere pattern, which for its part had been eaten by generations of moths. In the kitchen, the tin and copper pots were still hanging above the stone sink. In the living room, we found sofas and armchairs with petit-point stitching, along with a huge black-and-white television set. Wherever I looked I saw cobwebs of a thickness and size that I had never set eyes upon before.

The house was a time capsule of the world in which three generations of an ordinary middle-class family had lived. While comfortable, they were not rich; for them, parsimony was very much a watch word. The house also evokes those rhythms and traditions that were characteristic of the unpretentious, hard-working culture which made it possible – thanks to the heroic efforts of her sons and daughters – for Italy to become a unified nation. It is a story that FAI decided immediately, without the slightest hesitation, that it simply had to tell.

Marco Magnifico

Marco Magnifico

Located in the centre of Morazzone, a small village in the province of Varese, Casa Macchi is a typical nineteenth-century Lombard residence. The layout original structure, consisting of a two-storey building with turret, dates back to the seventeenth century, when the complex belonged to the Marquises Viani, one of the most powerful families of Morazzone. Subsequently, the building underwent numerous structural modifications until, in 1898, it became the property of Adele Bottelli, married to Giuseppe Macchi. Equipped with an elegant portico with stone columns which leads upstairs to a bright veranda, Casa Macchi demonstrates from the first glance that it has preserved intact the charm of a bourgeois residence at the turn of the nineteenth and twentieth centuries. In 2015, it was bequeathed to FAI by Maria Luisa Macchi (1924–2015), Adele's granddaughter, with the wish that it could become "a living museum" to give "lustre to Morazzone". The main door overlooks the main square of Morazzone, the hub of village life, where stands the church dedicated to the patron Saint Ambrose. The village is the subject of a important urban redevelopment plan aimed to revitalise small historic centres in the province. To contribute to the project, FAI has decided to open a small shop in one of the premises belonging to the property: the Emporio di Casa Macchi, thanks also to the support of the Municipality of Morazzone, the Lombardy Region and the Cariplo Foundation, gives new life to an old shop, restored and refurbished with furniture recovered from an old grocery store in Milan.

The exterior of the house conveys the typical atmosphere of villas of the period, equipped with protected and reserved spaces in which to take refuge, stroll, read and take care of the greenery and flowers. Beyond the garden with its gravel courtyard, the flower beds, the palm grove, the bamboo grove, the aviary, and the well, the complex also includes a large area, known as the "pratone" or "chioso" (from the Latin *clausum* or cultivated land enclosed by walls or by hedges), once also intended for agricultural functions. This is confirmed by the presence of a rustic building, a lemon house and a small greenhouse.

The charm of Casa Macchi has been protected over the years by Maria Luisa, who lived here for a good part of the twentieth century together with her parents and her maternal grandmother. Inside the rooms, still furnished with family objects, an archive is kept – consisting of portraits, photographs, letters, diaries, and postcards – that makes it possible to reconstruct the vicissitudes of the Bottelli and Macchi against the background of the main events in the history of Italy, from the Risorgimento to the Second World War.

The entrance, marked like the rest of the rooms by a long period of abandonment, introduces to a world of the past, perfectly preserved in the furnishings and decorations, down to the ornaments and everyday objects. On the first floor, from the large windows of the veranda, one can admire the courtyard and garden, and a glimpse of the centre of Morazzone. The counterbalance to the view is the night area, which consists of five bedrooms, two bathrooms, a boudoir, a small sitting room, a cloakroom and a dining room.

Warmed by a large carved wooden fireplace and a stove, the drawing room was intended for family gatherings, leisure and domestic occupations. The furnishings belong to the Lombard tradition of the second half of the nineteenth century, in the neo-Rococo and Louis Philippe style, enriched by French porcelain, prints, framed fans and other ornaments.

The living room leads to the dining room, gathered around the table and chairs in straw model Thonet chairs, en suite with the sofa. The walls, embellished with motifs and faux frames painted in tempera, house a large fireplace of marble with a carved wooden mirror and a series of hunting trophies. The room also preserves a plaster sculpture depicting a young peasant girl with a wooden bundle made by Luigi Secchi (1853–1921) and an upright piano.

The domestic dimension of the house is well represented by the kitchen on the ground floor: furnished with rustic and functional furniture, such as a typical Lombard sideboard, it houses tableware and pots and pans that seem ready for use. Upstairs, in the dining room, stands a television with wooden case, of the very first generation.

Villa Della Porta Bozzolo

Casalzuigno, Varese

Donation
Bozzolo Heirs
1989

Watercoloured photograph of the Bozzolo family
in the garden of their villa, in the first years of the twentieth century

Every house, whether it be beautiful or ugly, large or small, has its own voices, sounds and smells. Casa Bozzolo, or rather Ca' Porta, from the name of its original owners, for me and perhaps for all those of my generation means the loud and imperious voice of Aunt Teresa, the barking of an ever-present and thoroughly spoilt dog and the intoxicating scent of *Olea fragrans* on a clear September morning. Gradually, the voices fade away; the older generation disappears and the younger one becomes dispersed. The musty smell of closed rooms takes over and disrespectful hands carry off things that seemed to have been there forever. What to do? Should one try to carry on somehow, making do and choosing the lesser of evils by patching up here and there? Should one abandon the family heritage, mainly consisting of memories, to people whose main object was to exploit it, turn it into profit? The decision got put off, day after day – but then delay was no longer possible.

Heritage and preservation. Here at last were ideas that seemed both personal and convincing. These two problems were for me – and my job is connected with a far more remote period than that which saw the beginnings of Ca' Porta – of fundamental importance from the day in which members of my family established their first contact with FAI. They continue to be so. But now these problems are shared by an organisation which has been dealing with them for years.

I should like to end by referring to a subject which frequently goes hand in hand with that of heritage and preservation: fruition. FAI makes it possible for former owners not to be completely torn from the house which they have lived in for so long. That is fine for us, and for me. But I should like to put into this matter of fruition, of enjoyment, something else, less personal and less selfish. Ca' Porta and its park will certainly in the not-so-distant future be admired by many visitors. But in my opinion its function must not be limited to that of a mere museum. It could be something more. The library of Ca' Porta contained, among other things, a wealth of documents on the management of this microcosm, dating from the end of the sixteenth century. This part of the heritage, which is at present housed elsewhere, could return to Ca' Porta, be properly looked after and become the basis of a study centre for the history of the Valley and even for the nearby Canton Ticino. So much for my dreams, which concern the future; meanwhile, I welcome with enormous pleasure the agreement made between FAI and the Bozzolo family.

Carla Bozzolo
on behalf of the Bozzolo family

Villa Della Porta Bozzolo is located in Casalzuigno, a village in the Valcuvia valley, in the province of Varese. It was constructed in the sixteenth century by the notary Giroldino de Portu (c. 1450–1544), the head of the Della Porta family. The property was formed by a small "noble's house" and adjacent outbuildings, of which today there remain the olive press and the so-called "Caminata", an ancient kitchen. In 1669 it was expanded and equipped with a showpiece courtyard, while the garden was overhauled.

In the early eighteenth century, Gian Angelo III Della Porta (1690–1745), Giroldino's heir, married Countess Isabella Giulini (1700–c. 1749). The two moved to Milan and transformed what had been a "farmstead" into a "villa of delight", intended for relaxation and leisure. Gian Angelo III entrusted the architect and painter Antonio Maria Porani di Cabiaglio with the expansion of the grounds, now layered in four terraces; linking them together is a flight of steps with balustrades, statues and fountains, culminating in the so-called theatre, a large lawn ending with a fish pond, created by the Varese-born sculptor Cesare Pellegatta in 1723. This eighteenth-century arrangement of the villa drew its inspiration from baroque models, which to this day produce a spectacular picturesque effect, constituted by perspectival vanishing points that stretch all the way to the "hill of the Belvedere".

In 1884, the villa was acquired by senator Camillo Bozzolo (1845–1920), who was a doctor, a researcher and a volunteer for Garibaldi. Casalzuigno was for him a favourite haunt: it was there that he met his future wife, Caterina Belfanti, and spent long holidays. His death marked the start of a long period of abandonment and plundering of the villa, reversed through its donation to FAI by his heirs in 1989; after its restoration, it was opened to the public in 1991.

The interiors of the villa were frescoed by Lombard artisans between 1724 and 1726, probably under the direction of Antonio Maria Porani di Cabiaglio. In the Ballroom, the architectural features of the jambs and doors alternate with their painted "copies", in a game of illusion between true and false that, starting from the walls, reaches the ceiling, in the centre of which there are the allegorical figures of Peace and Justice, flanked by cherubs; the fresco illustrates Psalm 84 of the Psalms of David, which states *Iustitia et Pax osculatae sunt*. Both figures refer to the qualities required of the Della Porta family in their work as notaries and administrators of justice.
The ground floor of Villa Della Porta Bozzolo retains a number of very old rooms, including the so-called "Caminata", a space characterised by its groin vault – a special type of ceiling with lateral lunettes – and its floor, featuring bricks arranged in a herringbone pattern. The name of the room derives from the original presence, in the sixteenth century, of a large hearth (*camino*), later replaced by an oven with a dish warmer.
Of particular note on the *piano nobile* is the Gallery frescoed in the Rococo style, featuring young women, genies, tritons, winged nymphs and sirens that look out from the upper band of the decoration, whereas under the frieze there is a series of allegories of the virtues.

Today, Villa Della Porta Bozzolo retains only a part of its original furnishings, the remainder of which were scattered or stolen before FAI became responsible for the property. Alongside the painted doors on the *piano nobile*, which were the subject of a rapidly-foiled attempted theft, the eighteenth-century four-poster beds also avoided being pillaged, including that which gives its name to the Yellow Bedroom, made of silk damask and richly decorated. Fortunately, in the Library, the imposing nature of the furniture discouraged theft, thus preserving the more than 2,000 volumes it contains, including a number of sixteenth-century editions of Pietro Bembo, Petrarch and Battista Guarino, as well as numerous seventeenth- and eighteenth-century texts, such as a 1779 edition of the *Encyclopédie* by Diderot and D'Alembert. In the nineteenth century, the older books were complemented by a collection of medical texts, due to the professional interests of Camillo Bozzolo.
These latter spaces constitute the core from which the architect Filippo Perego di Cremnago [himself the donor to FAI of the Casa e Tenuta Perego, p. 134] started work on the villa at FAI's behest, reinstating the feel of an inhabited home in the run-up to the opening of the Property to the public.

Monastero di Torba

Gornate Olona, Varese

Donation
Giulia Maria Crespi
1977

An old photo of the ivy-covered Tower of Torba, before restoration

In 1975, when Franco Russoli suggested to the FAI Board that they buy Torba, everybody felt very worried and doubtful. Later, Russoli tried to persuade us again, several times, describing the terrible state of the ruins of the old Monastery and the Roman-Longobard Tower and warning us that vandals were hastening the destructive work of time.

Prompted by his insistence, I decided to visit Torba so as to see for myself. I shall never forget that foggy January morning with its leaden sky and snow-covered countryside. What I saw was so depressing that I went back and told the Board my serious doubts over the advisability of making the purchase.

But Russoli was obdurate and continued to insist; in the end, with his innate charm and those extraordinary blue eyes, he succeeded in making me change my mind.

"What", he would say, "don't you want to save one of the last remnants of Longobard painting? And those stones worn away by time, don't you want to tear the ivy off them? And those nuns' faces just visible on the limewashed walls, don't you want to bring them to light?" In this way, when I was still only half convinced of the idea myself, he bludgeoned me into buying Torba so as to give it to FAI.

The years went by and rescue work began. A large number of people collaborated, all with great enthusiasm.

The results are there to be seen. Torba has come back to life. Numerous activities of every sort take place there every year. For FAI, Torba has become an example of how to carry out an environmental rescue operation discreetly and with relatively few funds. But I should like to add that something else besides life has come back to Torba. The subtle, quiet poetry that emanates from its walls and that deep sense of peace give moments of profound reflection to all who visit it.

Thank you, Franco Russoli. We owe it all to you.

Giulia Maria Mozzoni Crespi

Giulia Maria Mozzoni Crespi

FAI's first-ever property, the *Monastero di Torba* (Torba Monastery), is to be found just a few miles outside Varese, and is an intact piece of the historic landscape overlooking the valley of the river Olona. It is located at the edge of a thick woodland, on the slopes of the high ground that had once been the site of a late-Roman *castrum* and, later, of the Longobard city of Castelseprio, of which Torba was a part.
Initially, the Romans had chosen the area to defend Italy thanks to its strategic position above the valley, the river and the road that from the north, beyond the Alps, brought goods, men and armies to Milan, which at the time was the capital of the Roman Empire. It was in the fifth and sixth centuries that the Romans had built surrounding walls and towers there.
The Torba tower is one of the rare remaining testaments to late-Roman defensive architecture in northern Italy, and is the most monumental element of the entire complex. This powerful, square-plan bulwark, measuring 8 metres per side and today reaching a height of around 18 metres, is the largest fortification of Castelseprio and the only one still standing.
By the eighth century, when it was no longer serving a defensive purpose, Torba became a religious centre with the settlement there of a group of cloistered Benedictine nuns, who raised up and transformed the tower into a liturgical space, and also built the nunnery and the small church with cobbles, bricks and ancient pieces of stone, some of which were re-used (the currently visible apse dates from the thirteenth century and replaced the original).

For around seven centuries, a female religious community inhabited this place, handing down as a legacy of their many years there the frescoes painted by local artisans that embellish the second floor of the tower, used by the nuns as an oratory, where we can still see the image of Christ in the act of blessing flanked by two angels, the figure of the Virgin with Child, and two orders of figures represented in a scene of intercession: a group of female saints above and a line of nuns below, portrayed frontally with one hand open in a sign of prayer and the other holding a cross. The first floor of the tower, originally serving as a sepulchre, underwent considerable damage through its transformation into a kitchen during the farming period. The only remaining depiction of the nuns buried in the tower is the fascinating face of Aliberga. The complex operation to salvage and restore the paintings was entrusted to the Milanese restorer Pinin Brambilla Barcilon (1925–2020), firstly in 1978 and then again in 2007 and in 2019, shortly before she passed away.

In 1799, the nuns moved away once and for all, marking the start of a period of slow decline that saw the complex turned into a farm and the church into a stable and a hayloft. The gradual dereliction continued until 1976, when the site was acquired by Giulia Maria Mozzoni Crespi with a view to donating it to FAI, which – at the end of the necessary restoration works – opened it to the public in 1986.
Together with Castelseprio, Torba has belonged since 2011 to the UNESCO serial site of the Longobards in Italy, and since 2013 the numerous excavation campaigns, undertaken in partnership with the University of Padua, have added content and value to the property, fully revealing Torba's true nature as an archaeological site of primary importance for gleaning an understanding of the most ancient history of the territory.
One of the most interesting archaeological discoveries concerns the tomb of a horse dating from the mid-sixth century, at the entrance to the tower. It may be a ritual burial of horse and rider, symbolising the high rank of the Longobard warrior – a practice that was still very widespread in the mid-sixth century; alternatively, it may be connected to a propitiatory rite whereby the Longobard community of Castelseprio-Torba renounced something precious – in this case, a costly horse – in exchange for divine protection of the tower and the walls.
Another significant archaeological find was the so-called "Blacksmith's House", a square building sited behind the surrounding walls, facing outwards, and constructed in all likelihood from the tenth century onwards. It was given this name due to the traces found there of a small smelting workshop (probably used to create the tools required for the erection of the convent). Repeatedly throughout its history, the building had to deal with the serious problem of landslides, as earth and heavy debris were dragged time and again down the slope of the mountain immediately above it. To this day, FAI is constantly working to mitigate the risk of hydrogeological instability, which is intrinsic to this site.

Villa e Collezione Panza

Varese

Donation
Giuseppe and Giovanna Panza di Biumo
1996

For many years I have had the desire to create a museum in the Villa, opening the Collection to the public. To fulfil this desire, I have encountered the ideal situation: that of FAI – Fondo Ambiente Italiano. Part of the Collection has been located, for a number of years now, at the Museum of Contemporary Art in Los Angeles, the Guggenheim in New York and the Museo Cantonale d'Arte in Lugano. The donation of the Villa and the Collection to FAI has made it possible for this legacy to remain in Italy.

I have deeply loved this house, which has also been an ideal place for the display of artworks. FAI, with its two decades of experience in the field of preservation and management of monumental and environmental resources, will undoubtedly be able to make the best use of the Villa's extraordinary capacity to combine the past and the present, offering future generations the possibility to appreciate this place and the art it contains.

I would like to thank my parents, Ernesto Panza and Maria Mantegazza, for having made it possible to realise this dream, and I dedicate this monument to them, in their honour and in honour of those who built it and have kept it through the centuries.

Without the commitment of FAI President, Giulia Maria Mozzoni Crespi, of the unforgettable architect Renato Bazzoni, and of the entire staff that works for the preservation of a cultural and ideal patrimony – the very essence of civilisation – all this would not have been possible.

Together with my wife Rosa Giovanna and my children, I express my faith and complete enthusiasm in entrusting this Property, which contains a large part of my life, to the care of FAI.

Giuseppe Panza di Biumo

Giuseppe Panza di Biumo

Giuseppe Panza di Biumo in a portrait by Ugo Mulas in 1966 at Biumo, next to a work by Robert Rauschenberg (now at MoCA, Los Angeles)

Villa Menafoglio Litta Panza is located on one of the hills that surround Varese, known as Biumo Hill, from which we can marvel at the views of the city, the lake and the Alps. It is a time-honoured villa with an eighteenth-century appearance – embellished by a formal garden and large grounds complete with a lake – which somewhat surprisingly houses a globally unique collection of American contemporary art, put together by the final owners, who lived in the Villa themselves, Giuseppe Panza di Biumo and his wife Giovanna. They donated the collection to FAI in 1996, together with the house, which has been opened to the public since 2000.

The first owner, who commissioned its construction, dates back to the end of the sixteenth century: Ascanio Orrigoni, an important figure from a rich, influential Varese family; in 1748, the Villa was purchased by the banker Paolo Antonio Menafoglio, who altered its architecture and decoration; in 1823, it was acquired by Duke Pompeo Litta Visconti Arese, a descendant of one of the most illustrious Milanese families, who decided upon new works that he entrusted to the celebrated architect Luigi Canonica, who then altered both the grounds and the building, adding for instance the so-called Imperial Room and the outhouse wing. In 1935, upon the death of the Litta heirs, the owner put it up for auction, and it was purchased by Ernesto Panza di Biumo, a rich wine merchant, who commissioned further works from Piero Portaluppi, the acclaimed Milanese architect.

Upon the death of Ernesto Panza, the Villa passed to his four children, but the one who loved it the most and lived there with his family was Giuseppe Panza di Biumo (1923–2010), a passionate art collector and pioneer in the discovery and enhancement of works by American contemporary artists who have since become celebrated. From 1955 to 2010, he collected more than 250 such works, of which more than 150 are still on display in the Villa, encompassing everything from *art informel* to abstract expressionism, pop art to minimalism, conceptual art to environmental art, and organic art to monochrome art.
Villa Panza was his house, but his passion for collecting would soon take over the spaces of his everyday life, driving him gradually to transform the rooms – which he himself defined down to the smallest details, with in-depth information provided to FAI so that it would comply with his instructions – in a space of perfection and formal rigour that evokes less a home and more a museum; one that reflects and today bears witness to his aesthetic vision, his philosophical research, his art historical culture, and a particular talent in the installation of the works, some of which are site-specific, integrated with extreme refinement, extraordinary originality and a strict compositional equilibrium in the spaces of both the house and the garden, in a harmonious dialogue with the architecture, the historic furnishings and the surrounding natural environment.
From the start of the visit on the ground floor, we immediately grasp the sophisticated and well thought-out combination of ancient and modern that is one of the characteristics of the Villa: sofas in red velvet, antique pieces and sumptuous nineteenth-century decorations live alongside contemporary artworks by Max Cole (1937), Phil Sims (1940) and Ford Beckman (1952–2014) in the Lounge, the Billiard Room, the "Hornbeam" Parlour – a hallway of hornbeam trees that crosses the garden, prolonging the enfilade of the rooms – and the small Dining Room, the Dressing Room, the Empire Room, the large nineteenth-century Dining Room designed by Canonica, with sumptuous chandeliers complemented by the monochrome paintings by David Simpson (1928) hanging on the walls.

A monumental staircase leads to the first floor, which played host to the bedrooms, two of which are today given over to the works of Ettore Spalletti (1940–2019), and there is even a bathroom, designed using green marble by Piero Portaluppi in 1930 in place of the previous chapel. A gallery – with baroque floor lamps, a pair of fifteenth-century nuptial caskets, inlaid to a design by Scheggia, brother of Masaccio, and decorated with eleven David Simpson monochromes on the walls – leads to a second Lounge, a Dining Room and a small Study used by Panza di Biumo, with books and family photographs. These rooms, in addition to the historic furnishings and contemporary paintings by Phil Sims and Ruth Ann Fredenthal (1938), house a collection of primitive sculptures from Mali, Congo, Mexico, and Guinea – expressions of a classicism that is common to all cultures.

We move from the rooms in the house proper to the Outhouses, which were once inhabited, but since 1970 people have been replaced by a continually growing collection. In these spaces, which are not striking in terms of their architecture or decoration, the pioneering art dealer Giuseppe Panza di Biumo allowed artists who at the time were not well-known, such as Dan Flavin (1933–1996), James Turrell (1943) and Robert Irwin (1928), to express themselves through site-specific works. In a long corridor, Flavin sited 207 coloured and fluorescent neon tubes that, together with the installations in the rooms that overlook it, constitute the largest selection of works by this artist permanently on display in Europe. At the end of the same hallway, Turrell created a lunette filled by the sky, oriented towards the sunset, and a radical square skylight on the roof of a completely white room. Irwin produced a portal that opens onto an unglazed window that frames the garden and a disorienting corridor, where the sense of space is altered by an imperceptible curtain. These are works that recreate spaces through artificial or natural light, changing our perception of them, and thus involving the visitor in an entirely original and memorable experience.

On the ground floor of the Outhouses, in the Stables and the former Coach Houses, the Ceremonial Courtyard, the Greenhouse and the Garden, there are other works from the permanent collection (by everyone from Martin Puryear to Maria Nordman), but also works by artists – such as Wim Wenders and Robert Wilson – invited to exhibit at Villa Panza on the occasion of exhibitions organised by FAI following the donation; some of these are site-specific, perfectly integrated with the space, architecture and nature, along the path furrowed by the vision of Panza di Biumo, who never considered this villa to be a container of works of art, preferring to turn it into a work of art in itself – the work of the collector.
In 2022, Rosa Giovanna Magnifico Panza, the collector's wife, donated to FAI another group of 108 works which had remained in the ownership of the family, to be added to the permanent collection of Villa Panza, which thus becomes the European institution with the highest number of works from the historic collection of Panza di Biumo, second only to the Guggenheim in New York.

Villa del Balbianello

Tremezzina, Como

Legacy
Guido Monzino
1988

A nineteenth-century painting of the Villa del Balbianello,
with the Loggia and the Gardens belonging to the Collection of the Villa

I never met Guido Monzino even once, yet I feel that I knew him well, thanks both to my solid friendship with a part of his (quite extraordinary) family and to the fact that his house and garden are the finest testaments to that excessive and almost paroxysmal yearning of his for perfection – a dominant characteristic of his life and, perhaps, also the burden that he carried with him right up to the end, enclosed in his perfect, heroic solitude. Deploying that same great, spectacular, impeccable organisational acumen with which he led the Italian team to the North Pole in 1971 and to the summit of Everest in 1973, he orchestrated the restoration of Balbianello, where he encapsulated his almost superhuman exploits as an explorer and mountaineer. In the 1970s, the villa was a charming, rather rundown house like so many others on the shores of Lake Como; Monzino turned it inside out like a glove, removing that patina which – I can't deny – I do miss, but also endowing the villa with that sheen which today makes it one of the most popular destinations in northern Italy. As we know, perfection is not of this world, but for Balbianello Monzino managed to tear off a strip of it from Olympus; whether this miracle was for him a source of perfect earthly joy is something we shall never know for sure… it is a mystery that is lain to rest with him at the base of the ice-house in the garden, which is carved out of the rock of the Dosso di Lavedo, and before which there come and go, perhaps unaware, tens of thousands of visitors every year – unaware but nevertheless grateful, as they perpetuate, for as long as God shall allow it, the success of Monzino's final escapade.

Marco Magnifico

Marco Magnifico

When Count Guido Monzino died on 11 October 1988 he left Villa del Balbianello to FAI, with all its furniture, art collections, books, archives, the Museum of his mountaineering and polar expeditions as well as the woods on the Lavedo promontory and other appurtenances.

To allow FAI "to preserve, look after and carry out any necessary improvement on this historical and cultural centre" he also left to FAI a considerable "dowry" so that the annual income it provided could cover even major running expenses.

Another clause in his will bequeathed to FAI a large sum "to be used for its institutional purposes".

Lastly, Guido Monzino expressed the wish that "FAI should always keep the Italian flag flying on the jetty at Balbianello, in memory of all the flags my Alpine guides flew in many parts of the world, in a spirit of idealism, with humility but always with heroism."

Villa del Balbianello is sited on the Dosso di Lavedo, a wooded promontory on the western shore of Lake Como. The complex is composed of the eighteenth-century loggia and the main section of the house, which was erected for the most part in the nineteenth century on the ruins of a thirteenth-century Franciscan monastery. The close unity of buildings and garden makes the most of the privileged position on the lake, offering what is still to this day the most stunning view of the landscape.

While there remains minimal trace of its monastic past, the history of the Villa can be charted more easily from the eighteenth century onwards, when it belonged to Cardinal Angelo Durini of Milan (1725–1796), who also owned the nearby Villa del Balbiano. On his death, the property fell into the hands of his nephew Luigi Porro Lambertenghi (1780–1860), one of the leading lights of the Risorgimento (the movement for Italian unification), who around 1820 sold it to Giuseppe Arconati Visconti (1797–1873) and his wife Costanza Trotti Bentivoglio (1800–1871), who themselves were fervent supporters of the Italian cause against Austria. Their son, Gian Martino (1839–1876) was an erudite orientalist: he married a Frenchwoman, Marie Peyrat (1840–1923), who was young, emancipated and anti-clerical, and it was she who, at the end of the First World War, sold the Villa to an American General, Butler Ames (1871–1954). In 1974, ownership passed to the Milanese entrepreneur and explorer Guido Monzino (1928–1988), who decided to leave it to FAI upon his death. Myriad guests stayed at the Villa over the years, including the man of letters Giuseppe Parini (1729–1799), who dedicated an ode to it, and the patriot Silvio Pellico (1789–1854), who enjoyed peaceful moments here as the tutor to the children of Luigi Porro Lambertenghi.

Villa del Balbianello is surrounded by extensive grounds, which were particularly challenging to create due to the shape of the land, constituted by a steep, rocky promontory, with hardly any cultivatable sections. Even today, the green areas of the Villa rise upwards, starting from the pier, with its large candelabra-pruned sycamores, to the wide balcony, demarcated by lower box and laurel hedging. The specific microclimate of the promontory has enabled a variety of botanical species to thrive together in the same environment: Alpine flora in the northern part and Mediterranean vegetation on the opposite, sunnier side. Of particular note is the "umbrella" pruning of the large holly oak that dominates the garden, which was requested by Guido Monzino so that he could admire the summit of Mount Legnone from the window of his office; this type of pruning is still used by the Villa's gardeners, who cut the branches using mountaineering harnesses.

The Loggia built at the behest of Cardinal Durini is the true architectural innovation of Villa del Balbianello. Supported by arches and columns covered in *Ficus repens*, and crowned by the coat of arms of the Arconati Visconti, it offers a dual view of the lake: Tremezzina on the one side, with the basin of Comacina island on the other. The Loggia is flanked by two rooms: a Music Room – transformed by Guido Monzino into a space for displaying the maps of his expeditions – and a Library, which today houses his significant collection of books on mountaineering and geography. The Library also contains a valuable rug made in Agra (northern India) in the nineteenth century, decorated with motifs of stylised palmettes and serrated leaves.

The only indications of the Villa's nineteenth-century past are the marble jambs of the doors and the elaborate handles of the windows. The rooms themselves clearly betray the input of Guido Monzino, who in the 1970s decided to adorn his Villa with an extensive group of eighteenth-century French furnishings. Alongside elegant and valuable furniture, there are other artefacts of non-European art (of African, pre-Columbian, Egyptian, Arcadian, and Inuit origin), as well as collections of prints with views of Lake Como, important eighteenth-century paintings on glass and Chinese ceramics, mostly dating from the Tang (618–907) dynasty and the Qing dynasty's Chien Lung period (1736–1795).

The specific location of the Villa, backed against the promontory of Lavedo, necessitated an internal pathway descending down the five floors of the house. On the entry floor, we come to Monzino's Study, furnished with French Louis XV pieces and a late nineteenth-century Agra rug, along with a number of fragments of rock brought back from the peak of Everest by guides Mirko Minuzzo and Lhakpa Tenzing, to commemorate the expedition organised by the Milanese explorer in 1973.

In the attic, Monzino wanted to put together his very own Expedition Museum, with flags, photographs, archaeological finds and awards which helped over the years to build up a picture of his celebrated exploits. The pieces in the Museum come from a diverse array of peoples: from the Masai to the Japanese, the Berbers to the Tibetans. There is a great emphasis on the section dedicated to the Inuit, composed of around 300 statuettes received as gifts of friendship from this Arctic people, making it the largest collection of Inuit ivory outside Greenland. Especially noteworthy out of Monzino's adventures was his 1971 expedition to the North Pole, carried out with thirty Inuit guides and 300 huskies, which pulled sledges at that time still made of hickory with leather harnesses, as can be seen by Monzino's own sledge in the centre of the room.

On the lower floors, the Green Lounge and the room known as the "Fumoir" are covered in eighteenth-century panelling sourced from French castles, whereas the Dining Room is dominated by English furniture and collections of ceramics and silverware, again from the eighteenth century, as well as groups of Beauvais tapestries (seventeenth and eighteenth centuries). Heading further down we come to the small Guest Apartment, previously named after the owner's mother, Matilde Monzino Alì, a noblewoman with origins in Messina.

Guido Monzino left FAI the Villa as well as a large part of the Dosso di Lavedo, and instructed that his ashes be laid to rest amid the rocks of the ancient ice house in the grounds. Since his death, in 1988, FAI has opened the doors of his property to the public on a daily basis, ensuring that the buildings, furnishings and works of art are subject to constant, careful maintenance, restoration and enhancement.

Villa Fogazzaro Roi

Oria di Valsolda, Como

Legacy
Giuseppe Roi
2009

A vintage photograph immortalises a moment in the family life of Antonio Fogazzaro: the author, on the left, is flanked by his son Mariano. In the centre, you can see the round, wrought-iron table that is still positioned on the patio to this day

I, the undersigned Giuseppe Roi [...], upon my death, bequeath to the Fondo per l'Ambiente Italiano, henceforth referred to as F.A.I., all of the real estate that I own in the Municipality of Valsolda (Como), under the precise, irrevocable conditions set out below:

A) The Villa Fogazzaro Roi, located in Oria di Valsolda (Como), must retain this name in perpetuity. B) All of the moveable property and furniture and fittings in the rooms of the Villa [...], constitute an integral and permanent part of this bequest; it is my wish that they should not be moved from their locations. [...] Instructions for the table service for 10 guests in the dining room of the Villa Fogazzaro Roi in Oria di Valsolda [...]:

I bequeath to F.A.I. all of the items listed below, which are tied to the Villa Fogazzaro Roi and which are currently located in the so-called "porcelain room", in order that the table in the dining room shall always appear as it does now to visitors. Ownership of all of the tableware made of porcelain, glass and/or crystal, and cutlery and accessories made of vermeil and silver, is transferred to FAI, with a view to replacing any items missing due to inauspicious damage and/or theft.

A) A beautiful damask linen tablecloth, complete with assorted napkins, pale or light pink in colour; and a white tablecloth, again with assorted napkins, for use as a replacement.

B) A complete English porcelain dinner service, with a pale pink base and decoration featuring white/brown garlands and flowers, marked: "Etruscan Festoon".

C) N.B. At the centre of the table, there should be the large tureen, flanked by 2 rectangular openwork bowls from the same service, elegantly filled with fruit or flowers (which need not be real or fresh!).

D) 2 spoons, 2 forks, 2 knives made of vermeil and mother-of-pearl, monogrammed A. F. (Antonio Fogazzaro), for each place setting.

E) 4 "graduated" glasses: water, white wine, red wine, dessert wine; with grape decoration; for each place setting + 2 carafes for water and 2 for wine from the same service, positioned

ADD THE CHAMPAGNE GOBLETS: SI GRoi

on 4 coasters with silver vine-leaf edging, set either on the dining table (water and wine diagonally); or on the sideboard [...]

Giuseppe Roi
(from the holographic will of Marquis Giuseppe Roi)

"I have in Oria, on the shores of Lake Lugano, a little villa lapped by the waves, at the foot of a mountain cloaked in olive trees, vines and even laurel oaks, which no poet, before me, has sought out. It is an agreeable and peaceful corner of the world, of which dreamers and artists are so enamoured." It was in these terms that Antonio Fogazzaro (1842–1911), author of *The Little World of the Past* (1895), described his holiday home at Oria di Valsolda, a lakeside village in the province of Como.
The novelist, a resident of his native Vicenza, was very fond of this house, owned by his mother Teresa Barrera – who hailed from Oria – and built in its nineteenth-century form by his maternal grandfather, Carlo Barrera, through the combining of multiple buildings set between the mountain and the lake, and by his father Mariano, who turned the original garden on the shore into the current terrace-cum-panoramic garden accessible from inside the Villa.

The places, rooms and views described in *The Little World of the Past*, which is set in Oria, can still be found today: from the little terrace overlooking the lake, transformed by the main character Franco Maironi into the "lyric poem of the house", to the garden with the *Olea fragrans*, "awash with flowers and vegetables and perfumes of rose and vanilla", all the way to the small dock, where little Ombretta drowns.

In the 1950s and 1960s, the writer's grandson and great-grandson – respectively, Antonio (1906–1960) and Giuseppe Roi, known as Boso (1924–2009), the last owner of the house and the person who bequeathed the property to FAI – altered the Villa, redecorating the rooms in a new style, but without eliminating its nineteenth-century atmosphere, which can still be discerned in the Library and the Lounge, embellished as they are by furnishings, artefacts and photographs from other family residences, and in the Dining Room.

The memory of Antonio Fogazzaro remains very much alive in the study, where he wrote, alongside his masterpiece, works such as *Malombra*, *The Mystery of the Poet* and *The Saint*. Inside the drawer, on the bare wood, dozens of annotations bear witness to almost thirty years of life and work, from 1877 to 1904. These include the heartbreaking words written for the son he lost prematurely in 1895: "MARIANO! / Mariano, my Mariano! / All vanity, all passion aside / I gather my heart / in God and in you / 11-8-95". On the same day and the same desk, the author noted the completion of *The Little World of the Past*, "finished in tears".

Villa
Necchi Campiglio

Milano

Legacy Gigina Necchi Campiglio and Nedda Necchi
2001

Collezione Alighiero ed Emilietta de' Micheli
Legacy Alighiero and Emilietta de' Micheli
1995

Collezione Claudia Gian Ferrari
Legacy Claudia Gian Ferrari
2009

Collezione Guido Sforni (1935–1975)
Donation Clara Lavagetti Sforni and Bianca and Maria Chiara Sforni
2017

The Necchi Campiglio Villa in a period photograph, originally published in the architectural magazine Rassegna d'architettura *in 1935*

In Memory of Gigina and Nedda

I remember the Necchi sisters well: simple and unassuming, almost as if they wanted to excuse themselves for having so much money and owning such an important Property.

The house became the hub of Milanese high society. The sporting types, who would splash in the pool even on chilly October days and play ferocious sets of tennis at all hours, were equally at home as the more reserved aristocrats, led by Prince Enrico d'Assia and Princess Maria Gabriella of Savoy, who were regular guests.

Towards the 1980s, Angelo Campiglio passed away and his loyal wife Gigina, who inherited the estate, suggested to leave her cherished home to FAI, along with a fund that would serve to cover the cost of its maintenance.

In exchange, FAI would have to guarantee that after the sisters passed away it would open the house for the enjoyment of the public.

And a dear friend of theirs also lent a hand. Alighiero de' Micheli left FAI his entire parlour, to be displayed in an appropriate setting.

And so, once again, Gigina Campiglio came to our rescue. Though she was still residing in the Villa, she let us decorate one of the large rooms, with its own entrance – a perfect setting for the precious legacy.

Every time I go up the staircase and enter that ample and silent vestibule, lined in glossy, polished briar, an image of the two sisters comes to mind: Gigina, the flagship, advancing slowly and majestically, with her precious sapphire ring. A very wealthy woman, yet discreet and kind, followed closely by her sister Nedda, more submissive but the more dynamic, curious and lively of the two, dedicated to her personal hobbies, like modern painting, in stark contrast to the style that surrounded her. And all around them, like a precious protective shell, the house: silent yet welcoming, sunny, always open to friends old and young, frolicking in the pool that the Necchi sisters probably never used in their entire lives.

I will always remember them fondly. And so two exceptional legacies enrich the city of Milan and its residents, providing a shining example for everyone.

Giulia Maria Mozzoni Crespi

Giulia Maria Mozzoni Crespi

In Via Mozart, in one of the most affluent districts of central Milan, which to this day still boasts the lush greenery of the extensive gardens of its long-standing noble buildings, there stands Villa Necchi Campiglio: a country villa in the heart of Milan. Gigina Necchi (1901–2001), together with her husband Angelo Campiglio (1891–1984) and her sister Nedda (1900–1993), commissioned its construction in 1932 from the famous Milanese architect Piero Portaluppi (1888–1967), who in that same quarter had created the Planetarium, the palazzo with the great arch in Via Salvini and the *Albergo Diurno Venezia* (Venezia Daytime Hotel). For the Necchi Campiglio family, the architect designed a villa capable of blending – within an elegant, understated equilibrium – references to a solid tradition of construction and expression with witty allusions, particularly in certain details, to the lexicon of the avant-garde, adding to it with great compositional flair and technical skill, some highly original, typically "Portaluppian" touches: from the decorative motifs – stars, meanders, weaves and lozenges – to the precious covering materials, including "ceppo" (conglomerate stone), coloured marble, parchment and briar-root. The modernity of the building was also reflected in the services and amenities: the villa had a separate porter's lodge and a garden complete with a tennis court and Milan's first private swimming pool; its layout benefitted from clearly delineated living spaces and routes to be used by the servants (there is even an underground tunnel), as well as ingenious and attractively designed technological solutions – from

the internal lift to the high-performance frames and shutters, and the radiator covers with brass grilles featuring geometric motifs. In short, everything was planned out by the architect, right down to the furnishings and the choice of tableware.

The monumental entranceway – protected by an automatic gate that rises and falls from below ground – complete with staircase, projecting roof and large glazed doors, reflected the desire to exhibit the luxury of the residence, as per the wishes of the owners, who were rich Pavia-born entrepreneurs. Indeed, the villa was intended to serve as a backdrop for high-society life, marking their entry into the social circles of the Milanese elite.

The interior begins with the hall, dominated by the staircase, the walls of which are panelled with briar-root and which features a balustrade made from the same material, complete with ebony inserts, carved into a Greek key pattern. Only a few elements of the original interior design by Portaluppi remain today, such as the console table surmounted by a large painting by Mario Sironi (1885–1961), *The Shepherd's Family*, from 1927–28, which characterises the space alongside *The Dead Lover*, a gesso sculpture created in 1921 by Arturo Martini (1889–1947), dramatically sited at the centre of the staircase. These are just two of the 45 works of art today on display in the house and the garden that were donated in 2008 by the Milanese gallery owner and art historian Claudia Gian Ferrari (1945–2010). Her exceptional collection of twentieth-century art has found the perfect home at Villa Necchi.

An unexpected and surprising telephone call from a close friend one day in 2008 informed me of a radical change in the life of Villa Necchi: "Well done! What fantastic news about Claudia Gian Ferrari…!". I had no idea what was being referred to. "Seriously? You haven't read her interview in Giornale dell'Arte?" *"No…". "Well, find yourself a copy and read it asap! See you". I read it: Claudia Gian Ferrari, the legendary daughter of the legendary Ettore and one of the most astute, sure-footed and trenchant gallery owners in Italy, stated that she had decided to bequeath her extraordinary collection of modern art to FAI. I called her straight away. "Good morning, Claudia, but… why am I finding out this news via the newspaper?". "Ah, Marco, at last… I tried to call you, but you didn't answer, and so I thought that by announcing it elsewhere you'd then get in touch with me." Whether that was true or not I cannot remember, but nevertheless we met up very shortly thereafter, and we struck up a great friendship in her beautiful, cosy home where Arturo Martini's* The Dead Lover *– an outright masterpiece of twentieth-century Italian sculpture – offered visitors a warm welcome in a little anteroom. "When I came back home after my chemotherapy, that sculpture gave me the strength to keep on going; she, too, like me, had suffered a catastrophe, and we got through it together." For Claudia, the sculptures and paintings in her collection were very real to her, and after many ups and downs she had decided to donate during her lifetime – not, as previously reported, bequeath – her collection so that it could be put on show straight away, arranged in the way she wanted, at Villa Necchi Campiglio, which at the time was being restored. She did so on one condition: "Marco, I need to be able to go to sleep with my works around me now and again. They are my family, and I would like your assurance that, as and when I feel the need, I can still spend the night with them…". This was not an easy request to deal with, due to access problems, alarms, bathroom facilities… but in the end we managed it. Claudia slept in the magnificent "cloakroom attendant's bedroom" only on one occasion. It is now designated as Claudia's room, complete with some of her Issey Miyake garments, together with her famous hats in the wardrobe. Claudia thus lives on in Villa Necchi alongside her works by Morandi, De Chirico, De Pisis, her* Pure Fool *and her Arturo Martini sculptures including, of course,* The Dead Lover, *who with her sorrowful, resigned silence, here as it did in her own home, welcomes us as visitors, perhaps helping us to leave our everyday cares behind as we cross the threshold.*

Marco Magnifico

Off the hall are Angelo Campiglio's Study and, on one side, the enfilade that leads to the Library, Lounge and Veranda, whereas the other side includes the Fumoir and the Dining Room, served by a pantry. In these rooms, Portaluppi's input is betrayed by the linearity of the volumes, by the fixed shelving in the Library and the Lounge – which plays host to eighteenth-century china and silverware, from a collection donated to FAI by the Zegna family – and by the stucco lozenges on the ceiling (a typical, recurring motif in his decorative repertoire), but above all by the Veranda. Two massive sliding nickel silver doors open to reveal a winter garden with double glazed walls, including an actual greenhouse, for an immersion in greenery that is reinforced by the effect of the sofas and the marble of the floor. Of particular note in this room, between a Chinese stipo and a lapis lazuli table, attributed to the Milanese architect Guglielmo Ulrich (1904–1977), is *The Pure Fool*, a 1931 bronze sculpture by Adolfo Wildt (1868–1931), which was a part of the Gian Ferrari Collection, as were Arturo Martini's *Bust of a Young Girl* in the Library and the paintings by Marussig, Morandi and De Chirico in the Lounge.

The Lounge owes its current appearance to a modernisation carried out shortly after Portaluppi, which in reality was more of an "antiquisation". In 1938, the Necchi family commissioned the equally renowned architect Tomaso Buzzi (1900–1981) to overhaul the interior design, with a view to softening and warming up the modernist lines and minimal decorations with more conventional furnishings and décor, inspired by the tradition of aristocratic residences and aligned with a taste that was more in vogue amongst the upper echelons of the society of the time. For instance, the linear tables were replaced with neo-rococo console tables, and the modern sofas and armchairs were swapped for upholstered chairs evoking the eighteenth century. The "antiquisation" also applied to the Fumoir and the Dining Room: in the former, Buzzi created an imposing marble fireplace in the Renaissance style, whereas in the latter he changed the chandelier and hung large tapestries made in Brussels in the sixteenth and seventeenth centuries on the walls; Portaluppi's input is, however, retained on those walls, which are covered in parchment right up to the ceiling, which itself features stucco decoration with a landscape of sailing ships, plants, animals, stars and signs of the zodiac.

The upper level was set aside for the bedrooms used by the owners and their guests. The owners' bedrooms and bathrooms are arranged on either side of a picturesque gallery with a lozenge pattern on the ceiling. Particularly noteworthy are the bathrooms, which are generously proportioned and lined with enormous slabs of coloured marble – a typically Portaluppian element – alternating with mirrors. Everyday items can still be seen on the dressing tables, from the set of Bakelite hairbrushes with gilded initials to the collection of designer clothes, scarves and hats.

On the other side of the first-floor hall there are two guest apartments, which today house two important collections. In the room where Princess Maria Gabriella of Savoy – a dear friend of the family – would stay, there is now a reproduction of the entire lounge from the home of Alighiero and Emilietta de' Micheli, donated to FAI in 1995 and installed here by Filippo Perego di Cremnago. The room showcases a collection of eighteenth-century *objets d'art*, including paintings by Venetian artists – best of all, perhaps, are Rosalba Carriera's *Portrait of George, Marquis of Townshend* and the extraordinary *Entrance to the Grand Canal* – as well as miniatures by Jean-Baptiste Isabey, French furnishings and clocks, Venetian mirrors and French and Chinese porcelain. Within the apartment, once frequented by Prince Enrico d'Assia – a painter and set designer for La Scala – the bedroom with furnishings attributed to Portaluppi and the bathroom separated from it by a black marble divider have been used since 2017 to display the collection of Guido Sforni (1935–1975), containing 21 priceless works on paper by Marussig, Modigliani, Sironi, Matisse, Picasso and Fontana, donated to FAI by the collector's wife, Clara Lavagetti Sforni, and their daughters, Bianca and Maria Chiara Sforni. The *piano nobile* of the villa houses part of the collection of eighteenth-century European porcelain and silverware donated to FAI by the Zegna family, well-known textile entrepreneurs who have always been close to FAI and to its mission. In the Library, a group of white porcelain figurines is displayed in a showcase.

Since the 2001 donation by Gigina and Nedda Necchi, the villa has been open to the public and today receives more than 80,000 visitors per year. An acclaimed house-cum-museum, as well as a venue for exhibitions and cultural events, it has become an icon for FAI and for the city of Milan. Since 2022, the villa's former garage, which at one time housed the Necchis' Isotta Fraschini luxury car, has hosted an immersive video installation that tells the story of Milan's environment, covering everything from the history of the city, bound up with the Navigli (canals) and the subsoil, to the modern interventions targeted at sustainability, which here – as in its other Properties – FAI is putting into practice to contribute to the efforts being made to mitigate and to adapt to the environmental crisis.

Casa Crespi

Milano

Donation
Alberto and Giampaolo Crespi
2013

It was Ezio Antonini, a great Milanese lawyer and for years an energetic FAI board member, who first brought me to Alberto Crespi. He welcomed us – as he had always welcomed his very few and select clients, including Enrico Cuccia – on the threshold of the back door of the beautiful family home on Via Verga; a sign of a style that gave no weight to appearances and had no time for social frills, but entrusted everything to the most rigorous sense of the quality of what counts.

Despite being the most famous law professor and lawyer in Milan – his best students at Cattolica invariably became princes of the Milanese bar –, he never had an office nor a secretary; he received (sparingly) at home and as long as he lived, his mother answered the telephone. Crespi, a great musician who had one of his greatest references in Bach (he had a mighty three-keyboard, 1,500-pipe organ built by the famous Mascioni from Cuvio, which he alternated with a fabulous Steinway and a magnificent harpsichord), played two hours every day and if a phone call came in those moments his mother's inflexible answer was "The Professor is playing".

His rigour, rapidity and wit of judgement, iron sense of duty, inflexible intolerance towards any form of sloppiness, approximation, lack of education and style and above all of intellectual honesty elicited an almost sacred respect if not often a justified fear; his judgements towards facts and people were peremptory, moral compromise abhorred. The discussions with his brother Giampaolo – who lived with him all his life – often resulted in a polite but fierce brawl; he detested Verdi and generally disdained melodrama; he accepted Wagner and regarded with amiable sufficiency the Romantics whom his brother, a violinist, loved and played; chatting with the two of them about music was often inimitable theatre for me.

He donated his formidable collection of gold-ground paintings, including the superb *St Cecilia* by Bernardo Daddi, to the Diocesan Museum in Milan; to FAI, in agreement with his brother and nephews, he entrusted the house built by his parents in the 1930s, which since then had remained totally unchanged in every detail, thus making it the mirror of that, now almost extinct, Milanese bourgeoisie, austere and generous at the same time, of which Alberto Crespi was one of the last great exponents.

Marco Magnifico

Marco Magnifico

Casa Crespi is a bourgeois mansion of the 1930s that has remained intact in its architecture and furnishings. The house was designed by engineer Erminio Alberti for the entrepreneur Fausto Crespi, who came to live there in 1931 with his wife and five children. The family produced metal furniture for offices, hospitals and ships, and the house, built right on the site of the old factory, tells the story, the everyday life of a self-effacing and cultured bourgeoisie wholly dedicated to work and study. Within these walls nothing has changed in ninety years. The few changes arose from the great passions of Alberto Crespi (1923–2022), one of his sons, a famous jurist, but also a great musician, who demolished a service bathroom on the first floor to make room for an organ, an imposing instrument of 1,500 tin pipes still functioning today. Again thanks to the interests of Alberto, Casa Crespi today houses sculptures from fifteenth-century Lombardy, seventeenth-century Roman paintings and many valuable antique books.

Palazzo e Giardini Moroni

Bergamo

In partnership with
Fondazione Museo di Palazzo Moroni
2019

It was some time in the 1980s and while we, as friends of his daughter Lucretia, indulged in some carefree dancing (as if we were on the *Titanic*) in carnival costume within the great rooms of his palazzo in Bergamo, Count Antonio Moroni – a wiry, stern gentleman, well aware that the times had changed forever – was weighing up his grand gesture. Within a few years, for the sake of his family's honour and for the benefit of the wider community, he would hand over – to a foundation that he had set up – the family home, complete with its grounds, its stunning kitchen garden (accounting for a full tenth of Bergamo's upper town!) and its precious furniture, thus depriving himself and his descendants of a prestigious, priceless property. It was a noble gesture made all the braver by the less-than-flourishing finances of the family; his two daughters (the elder of whom would die prematurely shortly thereafter, whereas Lucretia would undertake an impressive career as an interior decorator, artist and photographer) gave their consent, albeit unaware that a foundation without an assured annual income would sooner or later become another major problem. Lucretia, very much her father's daughter in terms of clarity of vision and lucidity of intention, brought her father's work to completion by proposing that FAI "absorb" the family foundation, of which, following her father's passing, she had become President. We decided to take an arduous road which, thanks to an excellent legal team, guaranteed that the Moroni Foundation would continue to exist while giving FAI full responsibility for its protection and management and, on the basis of an innovative formula, also its ownership. Antonio Moroni's decision, as noble as those of Gian Giacomo Poldi Pezzoli, Pasino Bagatti Valsecchi and Antonio and Marieda Boschi Di Stefano (to cite just three illustrious examples from my home town, though I could of course also mention the Panza di Biumo, Olcese, Doria Pamphilj, De Rege and Castelbarco families, who have all done their bit to help FAI), is part of that most civil history of our country, where there are still those who feel that a gesture in support of the community is a point of honour for their own name and that of their family; and as such, these gestures should be entrusted to the future and described just like the works of art and architecture that are the subject of great donations such as these – all very much in keeping with the finest Italian tradition.

Marco Magnifico

Marco Magnifico

Palazzo Moroni was built in the mid-seventeenth century in Bergamo's Upper Town, at the foot of the Rocca Civica fortress, along the ancient Via di Porta Dipinta. Behind the sober facade, there is a monumental courtyard, decorated by a nymphaeum with a statue of Neptune set in a thick wall that supports the terraces of an Italian-style hanging garden on the hillside. A noteworthy aspect of the Palazzo is that it has retained intact not just its garden but also a kitchen garden extending across 2.5 hectares, representing the typical rustic section of the ancient residential complex, which remains as productive as ever – an unusual, priceless slice of the Lombard countryside, perfectly preserved in the heart of the city.

The Palazzo was commissioned by Francesco Moroni (1606–1664) in the mid-sixteenth century, following his marriage to Lucrezia Roncalli (1585–1635): nestled amid the existing buildings, belonging to ancient noble houses, it was intended to manifest the social and economic prestige achieved by the family, who hailed from the Val Seriana and had rapidly acquired wealth through the local silk industry, and specifically through the cultivation of mulberries, on which silkworms feed. This is the reason why the mulberry tree appears on the family's coat of arms, which adorns the rooms; due to a curious coincidence, exploited by the Moroni, the family name is reminiscent of the Latin word for mulberry, *morus*, pronounced in the local dialect as "murù".

The construction of the building, designed by the Lugano-born architect Battista della Giovanna, lasted from 1646 to 1655 and can be charted, along with the vicissitudes of the family who lived there for four centuries, through the priceless documents of the historical archive held here and managed by the Palazzo Moroni Museum Foundation, established by Count Antonio Moroni (1919–2009) and today chaired by his daughter, Lucretia Moroni, who entrusted to FAI the protection and management of the building, which has been open to the public since 2019.

In contrast to the facade, the interiors of the Palazzo exhibit a typically baroque decorative exuberance. The eye-catching grand staircase, which leads from the courtyard to the *piano nobile*, was frescoed – together with the other large rooms – by the Cremona native Gian Giacomo Barbelli (1604–1656), on the basis of a pictorial scheme conceived by Father Donato Calvi (1613–1678), prior of the nearby Monastery of Sant'Agostino and author, in 1655, of a booklet entitled *The Mysterious Paintings of Palazzo Moroni*. Amid the illusionistic architecture painted on the frieze and ceiling, there is an illustration of the story of Cupid and Psyche, taken from *The Metamorphoses* by Apuleius, which tells of the passion between a god, the son of Venus, and a mortal woman, who is prepared to undergo arduous tests in order to marry him and attain immortality. The reference here is to the social ascent of Francesco Moroni who, lacking noble titles but thanks to his temperament and constant commitment, succeeded in gaining wealth and prestige.

The *Sala dell'Età dell'oro* (Room of the Golden Age) owes its name to the subjects of the frescoes that, depicting *The Metamorphoses* by Ovid, celebrate an epoch of purity and joy, reached thanks to the virtues. The figures are arranged within a complex architectural *quadratura* (an illusionistic painting technique) created by the painter Domenico Ghislandi (1620–1717), with Saturn dominating the scene from the centre of the ceiling. This room houses the Renaissance paintings from the collection, including masterpieces by Giovanni Battista Moroni (1520/24–1579/80): the *Portrait of Isotta Brembati*, the *Portrait of Gian Gerolamo Grumelli*, better known as *The Man in Pink*, dated 1560, and the later *Portrait of an Elderly Woman in Black*. These paintings entered the collection thanks to Pietro Moroni, who in 1817 received them from Marcantonio Fermo Grumelli, perhaps in settlement of a debt. Thanks to these acquisitions, the collection became renowned amongst collectors, art historians and connoisseurs around the world.

The ceiling of the *Sala dei Giganti* (Room of the Giants) was frescoed by Gian Giacomo Barbelli in 1654. The subject matter concerns the myth of giants, also found in Ovid's *Metamorphoses*. The so-called "fall of the giants" is here represented in a highly illusionistic key, thanks in part to the expedient of the architectural framing that "breaks" under the weight of the figures – an idea that refers back to the frescoes by Giulio Romano at Palazzo Te in Mantua, a clear source of inspiration.

The *Sala della Gerusalemme liberata* (Room of Jerusalem Delivered), which affords access to the gardens via a balcony, is the largest room in the building, and it separates the showpiece area from the family's private living quarters. The frescoes were inspired by the epic poem of the same name by Torquato Tasso, and represent an exaltation of certain qualities – faith, honour, determination – attributed to the Moroni, whose emblems appear at the four corners of the room. The frescoes were painted in 1652 by Barbelli and Ghislandi, who were responsible for the narrative episodes and the architectural framing, respectively. Of particular note are the two consoles, donated to the Moroni family by Cardinal Giuseppe Alessandro Furietti (1684–1764), an archaeologist and proponent of the first public library in Bergamo. Their tops are covered with ancient mosaics coming from the eighteenth-century excavations carried out at Hadrian's Villa in Tivoli.

In the early nineteenth century substantial changes were made to the original design of the palazzo, transforming the rooms used by the family to align them with the prevailing taste. Decidedly more domestic in feel, the nineteenth-century rooms are no less fascinating, embellished as they are by a stunning collection of paintings and *objets d'art*, including the porcelain clock designed by Jacques Petit (1796–1868) and four late eighteenth-century Chinese Canton vases – masterpieces from Palazzo Moroni's ceramics collection held in the Yellow Room. Adjacent to it, there are a bedroom and other rooms, including a dressing room decorated with painted scenes of landscapes and daily life in China.

The Italian gardens stretch across multiple terraces linked by flights of steps and are embellished by flowerbeds bordered by ivy and box hedges pruned into geometric shapes, and filled with red and yellow flowers, the colours of the city of Bergamo. The third, highest terrace gives access to the "Count's thinking place", a turret in neo-Mediaeval style, built in the late nineteenth century on the remains of a more ancient structure forming part of the Rocca Civica.

Beyond the garden, there are two-and-a-half hectares of *ortaglia*, a parcel of land at one time meeting the nutritional needs of those living in the building, annexed by the property in the eighteenth and nineteenth centuries by brothers Pietro (1792–1858) and Alessandro Moroni (1790–1869), the latter having studied the discipline of agronomics. This rare, evocative piece of country in the middle of the city houses vines and fruit trees: cherry, white mulberry and fig, and there is even a field of potatoes. The kitchen garden includes a *roccolo*, a circle of hornbeam trees whose branches are woven together to keep birds off. The fields, partly left uncultivated, are sprinkled with wild flowers and herbs that attract butterflies and other pollinating insects, making this an urban oasis of biodiversity, which is also being repopulated by local fauna, from birds to badgers.

Alpe Pedroria e Alpe Madrera

Talamona, Sondrio

Bequest
Stefano Tirinzoni
2011

Architect Stefano Tirinzoni had embraced FAI's mission with the same enthusiasm that he had towards his Valtellina; he was the first head of the FAI delegation in Sondrio and thanks to him the Castello of Grumello, which dominates Sondrio nestled among Italy's most heroic vineyards, was donated to FAI; he oversaw its restoration and donated the project. He died young, leaving unanimous regrets for his kindness and cheerfulness of manner, his profound civil conscience and passionate knowledge of Alpine culture. It was an absolute surprise to learn from his will that the more than 150 hectares of grazing land, which had been his family's heritage for generations, had been bequeathed to the FAI together with the beautiful alpine pasture complexes of the Madrera and Pedroria Alps and the two peaks of the Pisello and Culino mountains. Huts and alpine pastures had been abandoned for years by the Alpine Brown cow (the cow par excellence of the Orobian Alps) and by the Orobian goat whose milk, together with with cow's milk, makes Bitto one of the most celebrated and sought-after Alpine cheeses. FAI had never before ventured into the restoration of an alpine pasture, and the challenge was only met when, after a few years of study and after restoring malghe, baite, casère and *calèec* (stone enclosures covered only by a curtain), it was decided to buy back some Alpine Brown cows and Orobian goats in order to give back to these pastures (among the best in Valtellina) the dignity that history had conferred on them and only temporarily taken away. The first calf born from the initial small herd was named Giulia Maria, to the extreme joy of FAI's Founder; her dream of not limiting the conservation activity of the Foundation to historical monuments but to finally extend it to the world of nature and pastoralism had finally come true, thanks to Stefano Tirinzoni.

Marco Magnifico

Marco Magnifico

Set on the northern side of the Orobian Alps, within the Parco delle Orobie Valtellinesi, the Pedroria and Madrera allow the gaze to sweep across 200 hectares of pastures and uncontaminated woods, almost reaching the landslide terrain of the highest altitudes. The huts, privileged settings of the seasonal work of the cowherds who still today reach them leading their herds, are equipped with stables and cheese sheds, with typical dry stone walls, as if to guard the peaks that dominate the mountain pastures: Mounts Pisello, Culino and Lago. Numerous footpaths cross a wide variety of natural habitats in which the spruce dominates, allowing sightings of some species of Alpine fauna. After many years of collaboration with FAI as head of the Delegation of Sondrio and as director of works during the restoration of Castel Grumello, architect Stefano Tirinzoni, who died prematurely, left to the Foundation these precious testimonies of ancient mountain traditions.

Casa e Tenuta Perego

Villareale di Cassolnovo, Pavia

Donation
Filippo Perego di Cremnago
2020

I've been working with FAI since it was founded. The enthusiasm of my dear friend, Giulia Maria Mozzoni Crespi, for the noble themes supported by the organisation has always impressed and inspired me. Knowing very well the properties managed by FAI, I would never have thought that my farmstead at Villareale di Cassolnovo could arouse any great interest. Two elements in particular gave me the courage to show it to Marco Magnifico: my lack of direct heirs and my wish to imagine my residence, in the future when I will no longer be around, being protected and exploited in a positive sense. It was to my great surprise that FAI discerned in my home those very qualities that, by renovating it, I had always wanted to represent. My wish was to create something beautiful, suited to its location, that would make me feel in a comfortable environment. The desire to create a place I could escape to, away from the chaos of Milan, in the area where my mother Carla of the Counts Barbavara di Gravellona came from, always inspired every intervention and architectural decision I made. Precisely because it was a farmstead I didn't want to decorate it with important pieces or high-profile collections. I created spaces that reflected my personal taste within informal, familiar surroundings. This very aspect piqued FAI's interest, and they ended up convincing me that my house could serve as an example both of interior design from the 1970s and 1980s, and of the customs of country living on the part of a wealthy family. Today I am delighted to continue spending peaceful moments at Villareale, a place to which I feel very attached; I am also very excited about the project that FAI intends to carry out so that this property may be given a new lease of life, allowing it not only to be visited but also to play its part in the development of the wonderful area in which it is located: Lomellina.

Filippo Perego di Cremnago

Filippo Perego di Cremnago

In the heart of the Lomellina area, at Villareale di Cassolnovo (in the province of Pavia), near Vigevano, between the river Ticino that flows a few miles away and the expanses of paddy fields, there is a large, well-structured, typically Lombard farmstead, which had always belonged to the Counts Barbavara of Gravellona, the family from which the mother of the famed interior designer, Filippo Perego di Cremnago, came. In 2019, Perego donated it to FAI.

Lived in, loved, and renovated and furnished by him personally from the 1960s on, the house is the reflection of his signature combination of ancient and modern – classical, but with flair – which he refined over a long, successful career as the interior designer of the palazzos and villas of well-known personalities and rich families of the Italian upper middle class, starting from his solid background as a student of the celebrated architect Tomaso Buzzi (1900–1981). His input graces such buildings as Palazzo Invernizzi in Milan, Palazzo Colonna in Rome, Palazzo Mocenigo in Venice and Villa Invernizzi in Trenzanesio (Rodano, Milan), while his international commissions included the Rizzoli bookstores in New York and the Mila Schön stores in Japan, as well as numerous FAI residences. The houses on which the architect lavished his care and attention are examples of a return to a classical idiom, albeit simplified and translated into a modern and contemporary key, enriched by an

extreme quality of craftsmanship expressed in the various fields of decoration, even encompassing fabrics that he himself designed.

Building on the house's nineteenth-century layout, Perego enlarged it with two wings of porticos transformed into long verandas, embellished with gardens featuring rows of magnolias that frame the perspective towards the Ticino, with the main facade softened by a faux dovecote tower, to make it resemble more closely a country villa than an old Lombard farmstead (while retaining its rustic traits). From the original farm manager's house, Perego decided to retain the large courtyard to the rear and the outbuildings in the fields, for use in the farming operations that characterise the estate, comprising 48 hectares of land, 36 of them constituted by rice fields.

The house has twenty-two rooms. The ground floor, which plays host to the reception rooms, is composed of lounges, dining rooms, a library, a games room and a reading room. There is a kitchen and also a pantry, with cupboards full of tablecloths, dozens of table services (for up to 400 guests) and an entire room dedicated to the centrepieces. Within the homogeneity deriving from the orchestration of the project by a single expert, variety is key to the style of the house: every room has its character and its colour, and each is a multifaceted ensemble of complementary furnishings – brought together in an original, rigorous way – and objects, more than 2,000 in total, including family mementos, souvenirs from around the world, and actual collections, including that of paintings and sculptures of dogs, scattered throughout the various rooms. These diverse collections encapsulate the history of residential tastes across the twentieth century. Nothing was left to chance: from the upholstery of the sofas and armchairs to their arrangement within the rooms, from the lights to the wooden radiator covers with their grid patterns, and from the curtains and the curtain rails all the way to the rugs. Perego's particular passion and expertise in the design of textile elements and their combination is most evident on the first floor, where there are seven bedrooms and six bathrooms. In every room, the furnishings, coverings and fabrics boast matching colours and patterns, including not only the curtains but even the bedlinen and the towels.

Castello di Avio

Sabbionara d’Avio, Trento

Donation
Emanuela Di Castelbarco Pindemonte Rezzonico
1977

A collodion plate photograph of the Castle of Sabbionara d'Avio taken between 1862 and 1880 by photographer G.B. Unterveger, shows certain features that have since disappeared, for instance, the south-west tower of the Baronial Palace which crumbled in 1893.

The world has changed so much that nowadays it is often very hard for private owners to preserve properties of real artistic importance which are part of their country's history.

When the Fondo Ambiente Italiano was founded in Italy, with the same objectives as the National Trust in England, and the founders asked me if I was prepared to make the historical Avio Castle the first donation, I considered the proposal for a long time.

I had absolutely no desire to sell the Castle, which I love dearly for sentimental and family reasons. At the same time, I had seen how friends in England who loved their family properties had succeeded in keeping them alive by giving them to the National Trust. And so I decided that I could not give the Castle to a more ideal organisation than FAI.

FAI would be able to carry out restoration work so as to stop the Castle from falling into ruin and preserve it for future generations, thus continuing on a larger scale the efforts begun by my father (who had spent the last twenty years of his life living there) and carried on later by myself.

In this way, I should be able to make this historical and artistic treasure, which deserves to be known to all, accessible to the public, without however foregoing my own and my descendants' right to continue living in a part of the Castle, which I love so much and which has been linked with my family for centuries.

Emanuela Di Castelbarco

Emanuela Di Castelbarco

The *Castello di Avio* (Avio Castle) is located in Sabbionara – a district within the municipality of Avio, in the province of Trento – on the slopes of Mount Vignola, from which it overlooks the lower Lagarina valley. The valley furrowed by the river Adige has a road running through it that follows the path of the ancient Roman road, the Via Claudia Augusta Padana, a strategic communications route towards northern Europe, which in the Middle Ages was surveilled by a network of castles (or *castellieri* as they are called here).

The mediaeval military structure, built in a spectacular, strategic position, was later transformed into an aristocratic residence by the Castelbarco family, who inhabited it for more than 700 years. The earliest written reference to it is as *Castellum Ava* in 1503, described as a typical fortified town, complete with ditches and wooden enclosures, for the observation and defence of the territory; this building probably preceded Avio Castle as we know it today.

The complex is divided into an "upper castle" and a "lower castle": the former is constituted by the oldest ring of defensive walls surrounding the Keep – dating from the twelfth century – and by the thirteen-century Baronial Palace, in addition to a number of service buildings. In the mid-thirteenth century, the "lower castle" extended the original defensive system with an additional section of wall, attached to the existing sections and commissioned by Azzone Castelbarco (who died in approximately 1265). The "lower castle" includes the Guardhouse and the Picadora Tower.

Today, the castle is reached along a panoramic road that meanders its way amid vineyards, cultivated terraces and cypresses. The mountain massifs that surround it – the chain of Mount Baldo, the uplands of Bretonico and Lessinia – give the valley a mild microclimate, softened yet further by its vicinity to Lake Garda, which facilitates farming and nurtures the rich vegetation. Due to the extraordinary variety of its flora, Mount Baldo has been known since the sixteenth century as the *Hortus Italiae* or "Garden of Italy", and the Avio Castle estate itself is cultivated and productive, too, with a vineyard (where the native Enantio grape is grown), an olive grove and a vegetable garden, offering local produce to those visiting the Castle and guests at the Inn.

Sited at the centre of the complex is the Guardhouse, owned by the autonomous province of Trento and managed by FAI. This small, thirteenth-century building was originally used by military garrisons as a stronghold and storehouse, before taking on a representative function in the fourteenth century as evinced by the rich frescoes added to the two upper rooms, which recount the exploits of the Castelbarco family, providing a vibrant snapshot of the chivalric society of the time, complete with battles, painted curtains and geometric decorations. A large portion of the wall is given over to describing in detail a siege of the castle itself.

One tract of the path that ascends towards the "upper castle" skirts the enclosure of the sixteenth century Picadora Tower, which owes its name to the legend whereby this was the place where people were executed by hanging (*impiccare* in Italian). The tower is used by the heirs of the Castelbarco, who retained the right to inhabit it even after the donation of the Castle to FAI in 1977.

The route that leads to the highest part of the castle is a sophisticated defensive system, with five doorways, at the end of which we reach the Keep, constructed in the twelfth century. This is the fulcrum of the entire fortification, the heart of the Castle and the residence of the Castelbarco family.
The celebrated Love Room, on the fourth floor of the Keep, houses a refined secular cycle of frescoes commissioned during the reign of Guglielmo III Castelbarco, husband of the exceptionally cultured Tommasina Gonzaga. Amid various fantastical figures and animals, the walls also feature certain scenes of tenderness that have as their protagonists two youngsters struck by Cupid's arrows. The decoration is datable to between 1335 and 1345 and was created by an anonymous painter with an awareness of the innovations introduced into northern Italy in the early fourteenth century by Giotto and his students.

Over the course of the fourteenth century, Guglielmo III (?–1357), son of Azzone, had the Baronial Palace built, and made his home there, signalling the definitive transformation of the *castelliere* into a proper fortified residence. Alongside the palace, he had the church of San Martino built, of which today only a few fragments of walls and frescoes remain.
The Castle was badly damaged in the early nineteenth century when, in 1812, Carlo Ercole Castelbarco decided to reduce it to a ruin, both literally and in terms of the land registry, so as to avoid the payment of taxes; to this end, all of the elements that could be dismantled were destroyed, including the roof, the ceilings, the mezzanines, the internal staircases, the doors and the furniture.

After a long decline that began in the nineteenth century, in 1977 Emanuela Castelbarco Pindemonte Rezzonico (1934–2018) – a passionate connoisseur of art and culture, and grand-daughter of the renowned conductor Arturo Toscanini (1867–1957) – decided to open to the public the residence that her family had occupied continuously for more than seven centuries.

FAI allowed the public to enter as far back as 1978, following a major restoration. Since then, numerous other structural works have been carried out, in addition to constant maintenance.

Monte Fontana Secca

Quero Vas, Belluno

Donated
by Bruno and Liliana Collavo in memory of
their parents Aldo Collavo and Erminia Secco
2015

The Malga Fontana Secca in a photo from 1938, with the characteristic "pendana" at the bottom still intact

As one ascends through immense beech forests towards Alpe Fontana Secca, silence falls in the cockpit of the off-roader climbing up these steep and lonely mountains. Every now and then we stop and take a few steps to reach a clearing where we pay homage to the young men whose names are engraved on a grey memorial stone to remember their sacrifice during the Great War, which in the winter of 1917 here saw tens of thousands of fallen in the prime of their youth; 20-year-old Italians and Germans who, right in the trenches that still like great eternal scars, mark these pastures, lost their lives in the name of an ideal that we have forgotten and that gave us the supreme good of freedom.

Not only of broken lives and heroic deeds do these mountains speak, however, but also of bold pastures where the very name of the alp tells of a very hard life even for the Burline cows that with their black and white patches once populated the area, providing milk for the famous Morlacco, the local cheese. But the Duce disliked the Burline cows because they were not very productive compared to their cousins from the plains, which lacked neither water nor fodder; he decreed their extinction (but didn't he have anything else to think about?), thus incurring a popular uprising led by the wives of the shepherds imprisoned because they were guilty of disobeying the order to slaughter their animals; a magnificent story of pride and local identity that FAI will tell in the large reconstructed barn at 1,470 metres that, together with the dairy, the typical "pendana" and 150 hectares of pastures and woods, siblings Bruno and Liliana Collavo donated in 2015 so that this place, so rich in history and tradition, could become a destination for those who, travelling along the path of the *Alta Via degli Eroi*, will want to know and meditate amidst the silence of the woods; in the barn the story is told, but on the steep slopes of the mountain again the cheerful patches of Burline cows populate and feed these pastures that from afar dominate the plain furrowed by the Piave.

Marco Magnifico

The *malga* (alpine pasture) on Monte Fontana Secca and Col de Spadaròt is set within a panoramic mountain landscape on the Grappa massif, in the municipality of Quero Vas, within the province of Belluno. The property comprises 150 hectares of high-altitude (up to 1,600 m) grazing land and woodland, affording an exceptional view over the valley of the river Piave, all the way to Venice. This is a protected environment – safeguarded by the European Union as part of the "Natura 2000" ecological network – which is today suffering the effects of climate change in terms of the variation of the vegetation and in terms of drought, which as evinced by its name was already a characteristic of this place. It is, first and foremost, a mountain pasture at risk of dereliction due to its modern-day abandonment, but up until fifty years ago it would regularly accommodate the summer transhumance of the Burlina cows: a native breed of cattle that risked extinction after the attempt – initiated in the early twentieth century and then intensified in the Fascist period – to replace it with other, more productive breeds. At Monte Fontana Secca, the livestock grazed and the typical cheeses of the Grappa area were produced, including Morlacco and Bastardo. The herder lived and worked in three historic rural buildings that are still standing: the shepherd's house, the *casera* or "cheese hut", the pigsty and a large covered stable, as well as a second stable known as the "pendana" and now in ruins. The pastureland was deeply disturbed during the First World War, when Mount Fontana Secca was the backdrop to a tragic battle. Following the Italian defeat at Caporetto (24 October 1917), there were bitter clashes here on 21 and 22 November 1917 between the 22nd Schützen Division – which formed the Austro-German battle line – and the Vallecamonica Alpine Battalion, defending the Italian front.

The trenches and tunnels that remain to this day along the ridge of the mountain, right above the pasture, bear witness to this battle and those who fell during it. Alongside these ruins, there are also written and oral records, dating back to the time of the Austrian occupation of the area, in the winter of 1917: diaries, documents, ancient maps, letters and old photographs that FAI is compiling and studying. To commemorate these events, various engraved memorial stones are dotted along the path that crosses the pasture, starting from the *Alta Via degli Eroi* (High Road of Heroes), which in a few hours' hike from here leads to the famous military memorial monument of Cima Grappa.

Monte Fontana Secca was donated to FAI by Bruno and Liliana Collavo in 2015, in memory of their parents Aldo Collavo and Erminia Secco. The innovative project immediately implemented by FAI aims to reactivate the pastureland, with the reinstatement of the Burlina cows, to resume the production of local cheeses in the cheese hut, which will be restored alongside the house for a new herder. As is traditional, regular grazing will facilitate the maintenance of the pasture and the recovery of natural biodiversity. In the large stable FAI will create a visitor centre designed for educational purposes, with a view to welcoming young people and students, who will learn about the practices of mountain farming, making the most of both tradition and innovation, with an unerring focus on environmental protection.

A RICORDO
DEL DISPERATO DI QUI NON SI PASSA
DEGLI EROICI BATTAGLIONI
FELTRE PAVIONE VAL CISMON

Memoriale Brion

San Vito di Altivole, Treviso

Donation
Ennio and Donatella Brion
2022

From the first time I had the impression of entering a new, different and unknown world: that of the afterlife. A world that does not have the characteristics of the one in which I live and have always lived; a world that only exists here where Scarpa imagined and realised a piece of the Elysian Fields of the twentieth century. The relationship so different between empty and full spaces compared to the real world, the unusual architectural forms, the unexpected proportions between the materials – cement, stucco, majolica, gold, wood, glass – that make up or perhaps just decorate the whole context, the diaphragm that clearly divides it from the surrounding landscape without in any way excluding it, the unusual use of geometric shapes, pools of water, meadows, shrubs and cypresses, gave me and always give me the feeling of physically entering into the world of the spirit. FAI is grateful to Ennio and Donatella Brion for the great honour of having entrusted this masterpiece wanted by their family in order to maintain it in the best possible way forever and for all, as they have done to date.

Marco Magnifico

Marco Magnifico

The Brion Memorial is a monumental funerary complex located in the Trevisan countryside, near San Vito, a village within the municipality of Altivole, behind its small graveyard. It is a family tomb, commissioned by Onorina Tomasin in 1969 from the famous architect Carlo Scarpa to house the remains of her recently deceased husband Giuseppe Brion, an enlightened, Altivole-born entrepreneur who was the founder of Brionvega, a successful company on the cutting edge of consumer electronics in the wake of the Second World War.

This masterpiece of twentieth-century architecture was the final work by Scarpa, who wanted to be buried here himself, in memory of the commitment and expertise he had lavished on this project, which was amongst his most complex and significant. His own tomb, designed by his son Tobia – also an architect – with Fabio Lombardo, is located in a corner between the grand Memorial and the small village cemetery.

ONORINA·BRION
NATA TOMASIN

The Memorial was created between 1970 and 1978, the year of the architect's death, and completed on the basis of his designs. These form part of the more than 2,000 drawings held at the Archive Centre of the MAXXI Architecture Museum in Rome, which are a testament to Scarpa's inexhaustible creativity, technical skill and maniacal focus on details, materials and processes: an obsession that comes across very clearly in the Memorial and which is here resolved in a form of architecture that is more poetic than virtuosic.

Access is gained from the municipal graveyard via the "propylaea", a monumental entrance characterised by two large intertwining circles that reveal the interior and which are symbolic of the conjugal love on which the entire design is based: that between Giuseppe Brion and his wife Onorina, who are buried here together. The heart of the complex is the so-called "arcosolium", the name of which is a reference to the burial grounds of antiquity; here, it is a large arch covered internally by a polychrome mosaic with a gold-leaf base, under the shining vault of which the sarcophagi of the couple rest at an angle, eternally stretching out towards each other. Another three buildings are sited amid lawns furrowed by canals and ponds covered in water lilies, which evoke Islamic paradises and Japanese gardens, within an enclosure demarcated by a sloping wall that facilitates the vista of the surrounding countryside. The first of these buildings, isolated on the water, is a pavilion dedicated to meditation, deliberately positioned in sight of the arcosolium; on the other side of the garden, there is the so-called "relatives' tomb"; and last of all, there is the chapel-cum-temple for burial ceremonies, which is also accessible from the exterior of the cemetery, and features a large, round portal – it, too, surrounded by water in a garden of cypresses.
The Brion Memorial is a family cemetery, which the ingenuity of Carlo Scarpa endowed with the form and atmosphere of a large garden open to everyone. It is a place of silence, peace and harmony, pervaded by a deep sense of the sacred, and through the medium of architecture it achieves a dense fusion of sophisticated symbols and references, encompassing different cultures and religions, with a view to inviting everyone who visits it to engage in a universal reflection on life, death and love.
In 2022, Giuseppe and Onorina's children Ennio and Donatella Brion donated the Memorial to FAI, so that it could conserve and make the most of this key component in the history of architecture, which already attracts thousands of visitors from around the world, while safeguarding the site's priceless *genius loci*.

Villa dei Vescovi

Luvigliano di Torreglia, Padova

Donation
Maria Teresa Olcese Valoti
and Pierpaolo Olcese
in memory of
Vittorio Olcese
2005

The first time I saw my house was on a late summer afternoon. The long shadows underscored the geometry of the staircases, the arches of the porticoes were a play of light and darkness. The gate with its bishop's emblem imprisoned the garden behind grey bars. It was a magical place. My husband, as if trying to make excuses for this excessive majesty, explained: "Lots of people spend a fortune keeping a boat. I wanted to save a Venetian villa". In the Veneto Region, an association was formed in the early sixties, with the aim of saving the villas that were falling into ruin due to neglect. No one wanted to look after these huge homes anymore. They were too costly and often difficult to adapt to modern needs. People wanted more exotic destinations for their holidays. The new generations could not afford to renovate and the upkeep was too high, and so fountains, charming Italian-style gardens, "barchesse" (rural service buildings) and "broli" (orchards) all lay in ruins.

It was this spirit that made my husband purchased this, the erstwhile summer residence of the Pisani bishops in the first-half of the sixteenth century, from the Bishop of Padua. It had not been used for years. After a period in which it had been used as a summer camp for children, it was closed permanently. There was a farmer who lived in the orchard and tended the vineyards and the grounds around the retaining wall. We dedicated time and money to this building, certain that it was for a good cause: preserving beauty.

The choice of FAI is the logical consequence of the original decision. It is a great relief for me to know that this house, which expresses a rigorous way of living, where needs are more intellectual than material, will become part of FAI and that dedicated professionals will continue its restoration and protect the surrounding area, which constitutes its natural setting.

Maria Teresa Olcese Valoti

mariateresa Valotti Olcese

The Villa dei Vescovi is located on a hillock on the slopes of the Euganean Hills, in Luvigliano di Torreglia, a few miles from Padua. Built between 1535 and 1542 at the behest of the then Bishop of Padua, Francesco Pisani (1494–1570), it was intended as a holiday home for the curia of Padua: the ideal place where, having put one's affairs in the city on hold, one could enjoy recreational breaks with all the benefits of life in the countryside. It was a villa of leisure in the Latin tradition, and one that inaugurated the return, in the early sixteenth century, of the architectural model of the suburban villa of ancient Rome, which would later be developed in the celebrated villas of the Veneto. The site, moreover, evokes the ostentation of antiquity, in keeping with the tradition whereby it was claimed that the villa of the Paduan historian Titus Livius – the *Livianum*, from which Luvigliano gets its name – was located right here.

The man behind the Villa dei Vescovi was Alvise Cornaro (c. 1484–1566), the administrator of the episcopal curia, but also a refined humanist, an intellectual with a passion for architecture and archaeology, and a leading light of the cultural scene in Padua. In this endeavour he was assisted by the painter and architect Giovanni Maria Falconetto (c. 1468–1535), the first designer of the villa in Luvigliano and his closest friend, together with Ruzante, the celebrated dramatist who wrote in the Paduan dialect.

The villa has a square plan: it opens outward via two panoramic loggias on the *piano nobile*, and in the original design it also opened onto the interior, onto a courtyard that marked a return to the form and function of the *impluvium* of Roman *domus*, with a large underground tank for the collection or rain water, a solution set aside at the end of the seventeenth century. The building betrays the influence of the contemporary Florentine models – the Renaissance villas of the Medici – but also embodies the recovery of classicism typical of the humanistic culture of the time, which gave rise to the season of the Palladian villas, of which the Villa dei Vescovi is a groundbreaking forerunner.

The model of the villa-castle having disappeared, the Villa dei Vescovi is, in contrast, a place of intellectual leisure, to be achieved through the savouring of the surrounding countryside and the practice of farming, starting from the *brolo* – the name given to a typical vegetable garden/orchard in the Veneto region – which is an integral part of the property.

The *brolo* of around three hectares that surrounds the building is still there today and still productive. It is home to an orchard – planted out with ancient species of apple, pear and plum – as well as a cherry orchard, which produces a variety of scarlet cherry called *marasca* with a sweet and sour flavour, and a vineyard. One corner is occupied by the "frog" lake, which is also awash with lilies, aquatic plants and carp: another historical component that is an integral part of the villa and which today is showing itself to be a little treasure trove of biodiversity very much worth protecting.

A few years on from its construction, Bishop Francesco Pisani dismissed Alvise Cornaro from the construction site, replacing him in 1542 with Giulio Romano (1492/1499–1546), the eminent architect of Palazzo Te in Mantua. He was responsible for the plinth of protruding ashlar blocks that is a feature of the villa, giving it the imposing feel of an ancient monument, but with modern proportions and a modern sense of harmony. In the late 1570s, two staircases were constructed to link the *piano nobile* directly to the courtyard, along with a rigorous and elegant *parterre*, surrounded by a high wall with three large portals, created by the Istrian architect Andrea Da Valle (first quarter of the sixteenth century – 1578). The Villa dei Vescovi also benefited from the input of a student of Andrea Palladio, Vincenzo Scamozzi (1548/1552–1616), who was responsible for altering the facade facing the *brolo*, with an additional staircase and a typical, antique-style nymphaeum, a fountain in a grotto dedicated to Neptune.

The loggias are extraordinary, a refined and effective architectural and decorative artifice geared towards savouring the surrounding countryside. The arches provide a picturesque frame for the hills and fields both externally and internally, where they were frescoed by the Flemish painter Lambert Sustris (c. 1510–1584), alternating between landscapes with vine shoots and a faux pergola of lake reeds, and giving rise to the illusionistic effect of a complete immersion in nature.

The work of Lambert Sustris can be fully appreciated within the villa, starting from the most high-profile reception room, known as the "Room of the Ancient Figures": under a frieze that alternates trophies with landscapes, empresses and emperors are portrayed life-sized, as if they were guests at a banquet in a public room (*oecus*) in ancient Rome. The frescoed paintings depict mythological episodes such as the Rape of Proserpina and the search for her by her mother Ceres, who drives a carriage pulled by snakes.

Sustris was also responsible for the so-called "Putto Room": beyond the painted architecture there open up marine horizons, landscapes with ruins, lodges and little figures, while a *putto*, seated on the balustrade, is intent on eating a bunch of grapes. The subjects and the style identify Sustris as one of the few masters at the time in the Veneto who were capable of combining ancient and modern, blending the models of central Italian painting – seen in the journeys between Rome and Florence, between the ruins of antiquity and the masterpieces of Michelangelo and Raphael – with Venetian culture. Between mythological scenes and unreal backdrops, there are real landscapes, which were an integral part of the decorative taste of the Veneto of the sixteenth century: the countryside is ennobled and becomes an ideal backdrop to a "frugal" life that involves seeking harmony with nature, searching for what we would today perhaps call sustainability; Alvise Cornaro, indeed, wrote a *Treatise on the Frugal Life*, promoting that lifestyle, which was adopted by him also in terms of his diet.

In the minor rooms adjacent to the loggia – including the so-called "Bishop's Room", furnished by FAI with vintage pieces – the walls are painted with faux wallpaper, surmounted by a white frieze decorated by Sustris. The inspiration here came from Nero's *Domus Aurea* in Rome, of which the artist imitates subjects and forms that had been revealed in those years to the pioneering explorers of the ancient rooms half-buried by the ruins, called grottoes, hence "grotesques".

Over the course of the twentieth century, the villa's purpose changed time and again. During the Second World War, the curia made it available to dispersed families; subsequently, it was turned into a convent for nuns of the order of the Discalced Carmelites; later still, under Bishop Girolamo Bortignon, it became "Villa San Domenico Savio", a retreat for spiritual exercises and vocational courses. In 1962, it was acquired by Vittorio Olcese (1925–1999), in part on the recommendation of the art historian Roberto Longhi, who was concerned about the degradation of the frescoes. In 1967, in recognition for their painstaking work on restoring the villa, the Olcese family received an award from the Foundation of the American Society of Interior Designers.

In the 1960s, Vittorio Olcese was among the first major collectors of Francis Bacon, whose works were displayed in these ancient rooms. Thanks to the numerous cultural interests of the final owners, the Villa dei Vescovi became once again a venue for society events, but also a refined salon for artists, publishers, writers and politicians from Italy and further afield, including Dino Buzzati, who wrote of the villa in 1967: "It is located atop a little hill and its two proud loggias stare motionless at a singular panorama that is probably unlike any other in the world".

In 2005, Maria Teresa Olcese Valoti, Vittorio Olcese's wife, with their son Pierpaolo, donated the villa to FAI, which carried out a complex restoration project before opening the villa to the public in 2011. Thanks to this generous gesture, since then everyone has been able to visit it and to savour its spirit, at once ancient and contemporary. FAI has also introduced a café and guest quarters, which help to make the property financially sustainable.

Negozio Olivetti

Venezia

Concession by
Assicurazioni Generali
2011

The Olivetti Showroom in a photograph dating from the 1960s

Assicurazioni Generali is particularly proud to have made available to the public a place as unique as the Olivetti Showroom. Through a concessionary agreement, FAI will safeguard and make the most of the restored building.

The restoration project, managed and funded by Assicurazioni Generali in partnership with the Venice Heritage Office, lasted almost a year and saw the reinstatement of the Showroom's original materials, forms and colour schemes. Rather than being a one-off initiative, this project is part of the commitment towards finding the most appropriate usage for the many monumental buildings within the extensive property portfolio of the Generali Group.

It is no accident that the Olivetti Showroom intersects with the history of Assicurazioni Generali. In the late 1950s, Adriano Olivetti identified our company as the right partner for what was, at the time, a truly innovative initiative: to promote Italian-made products through a showroom in one of the world's most famous piazzas, and in the process to raise the profile of Olivetti, one of the leading lights of the Italian economy. A pro-active, responsible presence within Italy's economy and culture is very much part of the heritage of Assicurazioni Generali, as demonstrated by this tangible commitment in support of Italian creativity.

Indeed, Assicurazioni Generali is so closely linked to Venice that its symbol is the Lion of St Mark. The company is encapsulating all of its affection towards the city by ensuring the most appropriate utilisation of this intrinsically Venetian building, set within the Procuratie Vecchie, yet another symbol of La Serenissima.

Assicurazioni Generali has selected FAI as the property's guarantor. FAI is renowned for the rigorous, passionate and skilful approach with which it brings back to life and enables the use of some of Italy's most beautiful sites. We wish them great success in their endeavours to increase the appreciation of Carlo Scarpa's work and to encourage visitors to discover all the beauties of Venice, starting with those that are off the beaten track.

Special thanks go, last but not least, to the artisans, companies and professionals who, together with the property division of the Group, have succeeded in achieving an excellent preservative restoration of the Showroom.

*Giovanni Perissinotto**

Giovanni Perissinotto

* Group CEO of Assicurazioni Generali at the time of donation

The *Negozio Olivetti* (Olivetti Showroom) on St Mark's Square in Venice is one of the masterpieces of twentieth-century architecture. Designed in 1957–58 by Carlo Scarpa (1906–1978) at the behest of Adriano Olivetti (1901–1960), it is in fact a showroom designed not for retail sale but to exhibit the typewriters and calculators produced by the renowned Ivrea-based business. Embodying the company's style, the Negozio was intended to help disseminate its corporate vision and culture, founded on innovation and functionality as much as on formal quality and aesthetics. In terms of Adriano Olivetti's intentions – the execution of which he entrusted to Scarpa – for his company this was to be "a calling card in the world's most beautiful square". Closed in 1997, abandoned and transformed into a souvenir shop, the Negozio was saved from dereliction and oblivion, and transferred to FAI on a concessionary basis in 2011 by Assicurazioni Generali, the building's owner. Since then it has been regularly open to the public. For Carlo Scarpa, the Negozio Olivetti was a challenge, a long, laborious project, and yet he succeeded in masterfully transforming the narrow, dark shop unit within a historic palazzo – sited on the corner between the arcade of the Procuratie Vecchie, of which it is a part, and a passageway leading towards the canal behind – into a modern, spacious and luminous volume, compact and exclusive, and yet open onto the square and engaging with the city.

Beyond the entrance, signalled by the Olivetti logo – an endless spiral designed by Marcello Nizzoli (1887–1969) – we enter a space twenty metres long but only six metres wide, all full height but sub-divided by a mezzanine with a gallery made from slats of prized species of wood, accessible via a monumental staircase, constructed using blocks of Aurisina marble, which is the architectural and visual fulcrum of the entire composition; it is a staircase of modern regality – one "fit for a king" said Scarpa, thinking of Olivetti – that is exceptionally original in the design of its staggered steps, achieving an asymmetry that is resolved in a solid equilibrium. At the entrance, the eye is drawn to a gilded bronze sculpture by Alberto Viani (1906–1989), entitled *Nude in the Sun*: the figure of a naked woman languidly seated near the surface of the water in a Belgian black marble basin, as dark and glossy as ink.

Scarpa designed a plethora of other details that make this project a peak of his career and an exemplary piece of the history of architecture: from the mosaic floor in coloured-glass tesserae – a modern embodiment of the typical Venetian *terrazzo*, which creates special effects when submerged by the city's *acqua alta* – to the service door in Orsera stone, which rotates and moves on invisible hinges and which is entirely camouflaged, when closed, within the external wall; and from the eye-shaped windows, which through two sliding, wooden-grate shutters open from the mezzanine onto the arcade and the square, to the lights integrated into the rosewood-and-etched-glass panelling of the walls that give off an amber glow at night, which illuminates the arcade and this corner of the square.
These are forms, materials, colours and technical solutions that owe a great deal not only to their design but also to the typically Venetian artisanal expertise they manifest, evoking the lights and reflections of Venice and helping to make every visit to this small space a surprising experience.
Also emerging fully from the architecture is the vision of Adriano Olivetti as interpreted by Scarpa, encapsulating the "industrial humanism" that underpinned the success of the company through the combination of innovation and technology, and equally of culture and tradition.
The Negozio has been fitted out by FAI to commemorate its original function, with a group of vintage machines from the 1950s and 1960s displayed on dedicated shelves in the cabinets and on the gallery, as if they were pieces of mechanical sculpture, including the renowned *Lettera 22*, which is also on show at MoMA in New York, as well as the *Lexikon 80* and the *Divisumma 24* printing calculator, the design of which benefitted from the input of acclaimed designers such as Ettore Sottsass and the aforementioned Nizzoli. Frequented by thousands of students, scholars and enthusiasts from around the world, the Negozio Olivetti today also hosts art exhibitions to foster a dialogue between architecture, art and culture, which is entirely in keeping with the authentic spirit of this place.

Casa Bortoli

Venezia

Bequest
Sergio and Carla Bortoli
2017

The house of Sergio (1920–2017) and Franca Bortoli (1926–2011) occupies the main floor of Ca' Contarini, an elegant Gothic palace dating to the second half of the fifteenth century and overlooking the Grand Canal, right opposite the Basilica of Santa Maria della Salute.

The house faithfully reflects the typical layout of Venetian houses, with a long "portego" set up like a living room, which runs from the facade on the front to the back; at the sides, the dining room, the service rooms and the bedrooms.

The Bortoli couple were able to integrate with taste and harmony the eighteenth-century Venetian furniture with some modern pieces, enriching the walls with paintings of the Venetian school from the sixteenth century and eighteenth century and exhibiting in the rooms a large group of coeval Venetian, Italian and foreign silverware.

Sergio Bortoli embodied the enterprising and shrewd soul of the lagoon bourgeoisie, managing with talent the family business, in the sectors of electricity and trade of household objects. Together with his wife Carla, he decided to leave their beloved home to FAI, which took possession of it in 2017.

Casa e Collezione Laura

Ospedaletti, Imperia

Donation
Luigi Anton and Nera Laura
2001

Casa Laura at the time when it was still the Anglican church of Ospedaletti

I have often been asked why my wife and I decided to donate our Collection at Villa San Luca to FAI. First, there were no direct heirs. Second, there were thirty-five nephews, nieces, grandnephews and grandnieces, who were getting along perfectly well, with no reason to bicker, and this inheritance could sour the mix. Third, we are very pleased that the works displayed at Villa San Luca will remain as they are today.

We chose FAI principally because it is apolitical and because it already owns and manages similar properties with success, based on the model of the British National Trust.

Accords stipulated by the lawyers and notaries representing the parties state that nothing must be moved or removed. The Collection expresses the love that has driven us during the past sixty-odd years of collecting, travelling the world in search of what we were drawn to and loved. It is an eclectic mix, of course, with art from Europe, the Middle and the Far East, dating from 3,000 BC to the first years of the nineteenth century.

This is an unusual Collection for Italy. It is our fond hope that it may prove useful to future generations from a cultural standpoint, and in this sense, FAI seemed to us the organisation most likely to make our wish come true.

We express our gratitude to the entire team that will be entrusted with caring for the legacy, especially the President, Giulia Maria Mozzoni Crespi, who is perfectly in tune with our wishes.

Luigi Anton Laura

Casa Laura is a former Anglican church situated half-way up the hillside that overlooks the sea at Ospedaletti. It was constructed in 1927 to serve the numerous members of the British community who, from the late nineteenth century onwards, chose the province of Imperia for their holidays. Partially destroyed by the bombing raids of the Second World War, in 1953 it became the home of the noted antiquarian Luigi Anton Laura, known as Gino (1922–2007), and of Renata Salesi, known as Nera (1923–2021), who transformed the ruins of the building into a house-museum that is a veritable treasure chest for their collections.

Gino and Nera lived and worked closely together, sharing a passion for art that was nourished by constant study and research, which are reflected in this house as their most painstaking and heartfelt creation. Indeed, Casa Laura contains around 6,000 exceptionally well-made pieces, including Italian, European and Chinese furniture, porcelain, sculptures, maiolica, silverware and oriental antiques, put together with the insight of antiquarians, the knowledge of connoisseurs and the spirit of collectors, during frequent trips to European capitals or actual adventures around the world, especially the Middle East and the Far East. The result – a collection without equal in Italy or anywhere in Europe – makes Casa Laura a place so rich in artworks as to resemble a museum, constructed to allow the collection to "live" there even before taking the family's requirements into account, and designed by the owners with a view to arousing curiosity and a sense of wonder.

Luxuriant vegetation, including bougainvillea and other prized species, covers the facade of the building. Internally, the large entrance – the former apse of the Anglican church – introduces the extraordinary collection amassed by the Lauras, starting from an eighteenth-century Genoese sedan chair and a French Empire table. The most important piece of furniture in the home, sited at the entrance, is not made of wood but entirely of maiolica: an exceptionally rare chest of drawers crafted in Savona in the 1760s, of which the original function is unknown.

The Hall on the ground floor, entirely covered in Chinese wallpaper, contains two large stoneware statues from the Ming period (late sixteenth century), eighteenth-century French furniture produced by celebrated cabinetmakers – such as Oeben, Benneman, Cochois, Weisweiler and Hansen – and an extremely rare double-body cabinet entirely covered with Algerian onyx, presumably created in Sicily in the mid-eighteenth century.

Gino's Study is home to a wonderful collection of eighteenth-century Genoese furnishings, in addition to a fascinating panel portrait of the Blessed Giustiniani, attributed to Gentile Bellini (1429–1507). Behind the seventeenth-century panelling, there are numerous artefacts from various sources, including archaeological finds of European, Middle-Eastern and Chinese origin.
The large Dining Room boasts panelling on almost all of the walls. Made in Naples, the wainscoting features *rocaille* curls of carved and gilded wood, and houses on its shelves a series of Chinese porcelain pieces salvaged from a merchant vessel that sank around 1690 off the coast of Vietnam.
In the corners of the same room are two monumental "pumpkin" vases from the largest collection of china in Europe, accumulated in Dresden in the early eighteenth century by King August II of Poland. The other items on show include two neo-classical Ginori tureens datable to the end of the eighteenth century.

Worthy of note is the collection of antique furnishings, including the mid-eighteenth-century French tallboy, attributed to Mathieu Criaerd and sited in Nera's Bedroom, entirely identical to that found in the Dolphin room at the Palace of Versailles. Also remarkable are the pieces of Italian furniture, painted with eye-catching floral motifs or, as in the case of the Venetian pieces, decorated in *lacca povera*, or even with cut-out-and-painted prints, like those on display in the Green Parlour on the first floor.

The top floor of the house plays host to the Winter Garden, attractively opening onto the terrace, decorated with eighteenth-century painted Genoese furniture and decorated with a series of polychrome maiolica pieces, including a number of *trompe-l'oeil* plates with olives, lemons and cheeses, made in France in the late eighteenth century.

Patently not part of the collection – but curiously exhibited in a lounge on the ground floor amid a number of chandeliers and rugs – are two perfectly preserved vintage vehicles, including the 1950s Rolls Royce Silver Wraith with which Gino and Nera so often travelled around the European capitals.

With great perseverance, the Lauras succeeded in creating in Ospedaletti a priceless museum of cultures, which encapsulates not just a world of art and history but also sixty years in the lives of the two owners. It is a legacy that is to be found not only in the collection – tasteful and laden with curios as it surely is – or even in the house, which is evocative as a work of art in itself, but also in the spirit of the owners. They were old-school antiquarians, who dedicated their time and energy to beauty and discovery, driven by an insatiable thirst for knowledge.

Abbazia di San Fruttuoso

Camogli, Genova

Donation
Frank and Orietta Pogson Doria Pamphilj
1983

The San Fruttuoso Abbey photographed in the early twentieth century

Strange how things happen in life! Sometime in the spring of 1983 I got a phone call asking if Professor Ardito Desio could come by one afternoon. My husband and I were intrigued to know what a visit from this famous man could be about. Neither of us had ever met him.

The Professor duly arrived and the conversation immediately turned to Mount Portofino with all its problems, and to San Fruttuoso. He then asked us if we knew FAI. We had in fact not yet heard of it. When told it was modelled on the National Trust which we had long known and admired, we realised exactly what he was talking about. Gradually, ideas developed as we talked it over between ourselves during the weeks that followed. We had done our best to maintain the buildings, but with next to no income from the place it was a difficult task, especially as we had had some pretty large jobs to do on roofs and on the foundations of the Church.

My father, I remember, had fitted the fishermen's houses with complete bathrooms in the early 1930s, quite a go-ahead idea for those days. And when he had restored the Abbey bringing to light the beautiful windows, some of which had been filled in over the centuries, he tried hard to interest various religious orders and the Diocese to use it, but all to no avail.

Things had then lain dormant and time passed.

In FAI, my husband and I saw at last an organisation which could take matters in hand, had access to the necessary funds for restoration, had the will, the knowledge and the good taste to bring San Fruttuoso back to its pristine glory for the enjoyment of the public of today and of future generations. When we met Countess Mozzoni Crespi and the architect Bazzoni, our conviction that a donation to FAI was the best solution for the place became still more of a certainty.

We were even happier to discover that not only was FAI interested in the buildings, but also wanted to set up a permanent exhibition in the Abbey showing the importance and beauty of the local fauna and flora, helping people to appreciate them more.

While it is important to preserve man-made beauty, it is even more important to preserve life in all its forms. We wish FAI good luck in going from strength to strength on this excellent path.

Orietta Pogson Doria Pamphilj

Orietta Pogson Doria Pamphilj

A tenth-century Benedictine monastery, a fishing village and, for centuries, the property of the Doria princes, the *Abbazia di San Fruttuoso* (Abbey of San Fruttuoso), which was donated to FAI in 1983 by Frank and Orietta Pogson Doria Pamphilj, is located in a deep bay, between Mount Portofino and the sea off eastern Liguria, surrounded by a small conurbation. It can be reached only on foot or by sea.

Its origins are shrouded in mystery: one of the most well-known traditions has its construction dating back to the eighth century, when the remains of the Christian martyr Fructuosus reached the site by sea from Spain, accompanied by two elders. During the voyage, an angel ordered the believers to found a church in honour of the saint, and to do so on a beach overlooked by a mountain, right above a perennial spring: the water source was a miracle for the elders, a guarantee of survival and a manifestation of the sacred – and indeed, archaeological finds confirm the presence, even before the eighth century, of a human settlement, probably monastic, made possible thanks to the presence of fresh water. History and legend are interwoven in San Fruttuoso, because the village church, which dates from the eleventh century, is located on the very site of a spring, which continues to gush forth under the arches supporting the abbey: concealed for more than thirty years at the back of a restaurant facing the beach, today it is visible once again, thanks to FAI's intervention.

In 1467, following the death of the last regular abbot, the community of monks left the monastery, triggering the inexorable decline of the abbey, which would be safeguarded by commendatory abbots, belonging almost exclusively to the noble Doria family. Restructuring works altered the internal and external appearance of the church, and its interior was transformed into a home for the new settlers.
In 1551, admiral Andrea Doria obtained the patronage over San Fruttuoso from Pope Julius III, in exchange for the promise to build a fortress that would protect the complex from pirate raids. Due to his death in 1560, the admiral was not able to keep his side of the bargain, but his heirs, Giovanni Andrea and Pagano, did have a defensive tower built in 1562; it is still standing and was restored by FAI, which also cleaned the facades embellished by the family's coat of arms.
In 1885, San Fruttuoso became the parish church of the small fishing village, which at the time had a population of 180 souls.

The complex, as we see it today, encompasses the thirteenth-century abbey, the church and a cloister arranged over two orders. Most of the current abbey building dates from the tenth and eleventh centuries, while the characteristic sea-facing facade was added in the thirteenth century. It is made entirely from squared stone, with five three-light windows per storey.

The upper cloister was erected in the twelfth century and underwent a comprehensive overhaul in the mid-sixteenth, as part of the restoration works overseen by the Doria family. All that remains of the original construction today is an eight-arched multi-light window, which looked out to sea before the addition of the new facade section in the thirteenth century. The lower cloister, which is reached via a small garden, was reconstructed in the late eleventh century using columns and capitals conserved after the destruction of the existing building. From here we access the deep barrel-vaulted crypt housing the Doria tombs, datable to between 1275 and 1305, and made from white marble and grey stone, alternated in the typical two-tone pattern; arranged in rows on the three sides of the room, the tombs are constituted by brick arches, mostly with epigraphs, and they contain seven members of the Doria family.

Over recent years, FAI has completed major restoration works involving the church, the facades of the abbey and the Doria tombs. The abbey itself and the surrounding settlement are now permanently protected against the increasingly frequent damage wrought by climate change, starting from the disaster of 1915 in which a flood caused the collapse of the first bay of the church, the debris carried downstream by the raging torrent then forming the beach in front of the complex.

Casa Carbone

Lavagna, Genova

Bequest
Emanuele and Siria Carbone
1987

I name FAI as my heir, on the condition that my property on Via Riboli, Lavagna, be made into a local museum, so that those who so desire may come to know, in the future, how and where bourgeois families lived in Liguria, before the necessities of modern life depersonalised our homes.

Emanuele Carbone

Emanuele Carbone

In Memory of Siria Carbone

Siria Carbone – how could I forget her? Our first meeting left an impression I will always remember: she was walking towards me with a firm, military step, in command, holding a cane. It was not so much to lean on as to point the way, like a lance or a sword.

At first she came to our seminars, cautiously evaluating whether FAI was "up to the job", if she could trust these odd people who looked after assets and properties that did not belong to them.

She favoured the typical spinach and ricotta pie ("torta pasqualina") and Ligurian whites, which she would offer visitors to her home, a perfect setting for its resident. A friendship sprang up between her and Bazzoni, and over the years it grew strong and true. Now this friendship was extended to me, but in small doses, because Siria was wise, and she always knew the measure of things, never went too far. But she would come more and more frequently to our meetings, still with a watchful eye, ready to catch every detail.

Even when she fell ill, she would still come, more and more taken by FAI, showing more and more faith in us, and when she passed away, she left us what she had held most dear.

But let us remember the indomitable Siria, the intrepid and astute woman who is still with us, who speaks to us through her home, which so faithfully reflects her spirit.

The waves of wisdom and discipline that Siria emanated still resonate around this home. When a visitor enters they whisper: "Remember FAI, like I did, with a legacy that befits your position and possibilities…"

Thank you, Siria, for having left your legacy to FAI, and most of all, for having believed in us.

Giulia Maria Mozzoni Crespi

Giulia Maria Mozzoni Crespi

Emanuele and Siria Carbone
together with their mother in a period photograph

Casa Carbone is an elegant, mid-nineteenth-century palazzo situated on Via Riboli, very close to the centre of Lavagna, an ancient coastal town in the province of Genoa, between the renowned seaside resorts of Chiavari and Sestri. Originally owned by the Bianchi, a local family of marble workers, the building was acquired by the Raffo family and subsequently by the Carbone siblings, who in 1993 left the entire property to FAI. Following an intensive restoration programme, in 2004 FAI opened the residence to the public, transforming the ground floor into an area for receiving visitors and staging events, and working hard on an ongoing basis to keep the exterior and interior in a perfect state of conservation.
The three-storey building, complete with its small rear garden, retains on its facade the original wall paintings, with garlands and faux architecture, that are typical of the local decorative tradition.

The house was inhabited in the twentieth century by the siblings Emanuele (1906–1987) and Siria Carbone (1910–1993), following his inheriting of the property in the 1940s from his wife, Margherita Raffo. The son of a naval engineer with humble origins, Emanuele would enjoy a brilliant career as a banker, eventually being appointed manager of the Chiavari branch of the Banca d'America e d'Italia. In 1983, he requested that his home on Via Riboli be listed by the Culture Office, with a view to transferring it eventually into public ownership. Following the death of his wife, he lived with his sister Siria, an energetic and sociable woman who lavished care on the house and vegetable garden, and was active as a FAI volunteer. It was Siria who expanded her brother's bequest to FAI to include other artefacts, and also set aside other funds in her will for the maintenance of the property, in order to "allow those who want to know, precisely how and where the upper-middle-class families lived in Liguria before the demands of our society depersonalised our homes".
The interior decor of the house reflects the taste for revisiting past styles that was in vogue in what was an eclectic age. Of particular interest is the collection of paintings of the Ligurian school, dating from the sixteenth to the eighteenth centuries.

The apartment on the *piano nobile* retains its nineteenth-century floors and ceilings, as well as Ligurian furniture from the eighteenth and nineteenth centuries, and significantly documents the domestic dimension of bourgeois life at that time, in which a sober, cultured elegance was always achieved with measured discretion.
The reception room (the *Salone*), intended for the receiving of guests, features a ceiling decorated with a nineteenth-century fresco of *Christopher Columbus presenting American Indians to Queen Isabella*. At the centre of the traditional mosaic floor, our eye is attracted by the insignia of the Bianchi, the first owners of the property. The furnishings in the home afford an interesting overview of the interior design schemes that were popular amongst the *haute bourgeoisie* of the Italian Riviera in the nineteenth and twentieth centuries, as embodied by the beautiful extending table in the Salone. The paintings in this room include two impressive portraits of senators painted by Gio Enrico Vaymer (1665–1738).
The Dining Room includes a stylishly laid-out dining table, whereas the copious collection of French and English ceramics conserved here – dating from the nineteenth and twentieth centuries – manifests Siria's passion for objects associated with the receiving of guests.
The bedrooms are home to a diverse array of furnishings, as well as the personal items and toiletries of the owners. The art on show in these rooms includes works by the Ligurians Domenico Fiasella (1589–1669), Giovanni Battista Merano (1632–1698), Bernardo Castello (1557?–1629) and Giovanni Battista Paggi (1554–1627). Alongside these paintings by regional artists, there are several watercolours painted by Emanuele Carbone, himself a gifted artist. The variety of the interests of the homeowner is made clear by the books on art, astronomy, philosophy and literature found in the Bedroom.
A small, late-nineteenth-century lounge in the neo-rococo style, houses glassware, china and a delightful collection of fans made of mother-of-pearl and ivory, while on display in Emanuele's Study are not only scientific and astronomical instruments, watches and music boxes, but also lively marionettes that he liked to carve as a hobby.

Podere Case Lovara

Levanto, La Spezia

Donation
Immobiliare Fiascherino
2009

The Punta Mesco promontory area in an aerial shot of 1973

In the 1980s a real estate company from Monza, Fiascherino srl, bought 45 hectares of unspoilt Mediterranean maquis overlooking the sea halfway between Levanto and Monterosso; in winter, Corsica seems so close that it feels as if you could touch its snow-capped peaks and, on the right, the panorama (like a joke of geography) is closed by Monviso. Who knows how many inhabitants of Milan and Brianza, eager for peace, will want to buy a nice little villa here… But one bad, oops… one fine day, on 6 October 1999, the President of the Republic Carlo Azeglio Ciampi signed the decree establishing the Cinque Terre National Park; no more roads, no more electricity, no more aqueduct, no more houses. Nothing at all; only strawberry trees, holm oaks, dry stone walls and the olive trees, vines and fruit trees that crown two somewhat dilapidated farmhouses – the historic Case Lovara – which remain without a future; because in the roaring 1980s of economic prosperity the future, to be worthy of the name, had to be different from the past! Ten years after, a Fiascherino councillor comes into contact with FAI; the story of the new future of the Baia di Ieranto, with its restored walls, its olive trees once again productive and healthy and the restored rural dwellings gives him an idea. He speaks about it to his fellow Councillors and they agree to donate those 45 hectares to FAI, just as Romano Prodi did with Ieranto many years earlier.

Thus, one winter's day I climb the steep path from Monterosso to Punta Mesco to have a look at this abandoned old small farm and I knock on the door of the red house (the one in the best condition, the other much older one is half-collapsed). Out comes the old farmer in woollen knickers and unkempt beard who still, through a sort of inertia force of life, gives relief to those olive trees which, despite the change of ownership, he has always continued to consider his own. He lives alone because his family has long since chosen to move down to the village; but he cannot, and heedless of the multiple eviction notices he has continued to live with his olive trees, facing his sea, an hour's walk from the village… He opens the door only to shut it on my face, not after roaring at me, "You can't come in here!".

That day began the difficult and passionate love affair between FAI and the old farm that, thanks to the Zegna Foundation and the life force of nature, has returned to those good old days when the Cinque Terre were one of the gardens of the world; the two farmsteads and the hundreds of metres of reconstructed dry-stone walls conceal among the ancient stones the most modern advances in technology to enable the production of solar energy and the purification of rainwater for civil use and black water for agricultural use. The future has arrived: the real one.

Marco Magnifico

Marco Magnifico

Stretching out into the crystal-clear sea, the farm of Podere Case Lovara – immersed in the Cinque Terre National Park and reachable only on foot – covers a total of 45 hectares on the promontory of Punta Mesco, which separates the bay of Levanto from the bay of Monterosso.
These are quite exceptionally valuable surroundings in terms of the environment and the landscape, where wooded areas alternate with Mediterranean maquis and terraced slopes, shaped by human hands to enable such steep plots to be cultivated.
The area owned by FAI includes three rural buildings – the first, smaller property, called *Casa Nuova* (New House), being located along the path, with the other two, known as the *Case Lovara* (Lovara Houses), slightly further away – as well as woods of holm oak and pine, patches of Mediterranean scrubland and two streams that run together near the cliff.

In 2009, at the time of the donation, the site was in a state of complete abandonment: the buildings were languishing in conditions of serious decay, and the farmland, having been left unchecked for decades, was in large part covered in overgrown vegetation which had compromised the crops and which was also contributing to the gradual collapse of the dry-stone walls – traditional structures of the Cinque Terre area, which play an important role in combating hydrogeological risk.

Podere Case Lovara thus became the heart of an innovative pilot project, launched in 2013 thanks to a Memorandum of Understanding signed by Liguria Region, Levanto local council, Monterosso local council, the Cinque Terre National Park, the Zegna Foundation and FAI, in collaboration with the Italian Ministry of the Environment, which saw the parties undertaking to react against the neglect of a typical Italian rural landscape by reinstating traditional agricultural practices as a tool for the safeguarding of the territory, the prevention of hydrogeological instability, the activation of economic and productive resources and the incentivisation of a conscious form of tourism – one that is increasingly interested in local culture and respect for the environment.

FAI therefore restored the buildings intended to welcome guests and provide catering, hospitality and visitor services; it reinstated the dry-stone walls of the original terraces, planting a vineyard, olive trees, fruit trees and 250 square metres of vegetable gardens; it installed a number of beehives and began breeding bees. Moreover, it is still to this day experimenting with a range of sustainable technologies, with a view to saving energy and contributing to the wellbeing of the landscape and the environment, while overcoming the isolation of the buildings from energy distribution and water supply systems.
Podere Case Lovara aims to become a seaside oasis, fostering a renewed sensitivity towards the culture of the landscape and, above all, encouraging good practices for the eco-sustainable development of the area.

Villa Rezzola

Pugliola, fraz. di Lerici, La Spezia

Bequeathed by
Countess Maria Adele Carnevale Miniati
2020

Villa Rezzola in a historical postcard

Pupa Miniati Carnevale was an upbeat, intelligent, cultured, stylish lady – a formidable woman of the old school who modelled in her image and likeness that piece of paradise that fate had placed in her hands and which she, through FAI, decided to donate to everyone: Villa Rezzola.

Inherited from her mother, who used it as a summer residence, it was chosen by Pupa as her only home, and into it and its breathtaking garden she channelled her creativity, her taste, her culture and her love for that magnificent, celebrated tract of the Ligurian coast, the Golfo dei Poeti (Gulf of Poets), which from the terrace of Villa Rezzola one can savour in its astoundingly beautiful entirety. The spacious villa retains intact that domestic charm which English country houses tend to offer in spades, while the fabulous garden displays that extraordinary ability to tame nature for which English landscaping is rightly renowned. It is not surprising, then, that Villa Rezzola was commissioned by one of the many English families who fell prey to the seduction of the Ligurian coast, dotting it with wonderful houses and gardens where the owners would spend the winter. After the golden age that came to an end with the First World War, these grand residences were gradually abandoned, often going on to suffer decades of neglect. Mercifully, Villa Rezzola's destiny was assured by the decisive, practical and positive character of Pupa Miniati Carnevale, who breathed new life into it, giving it her time, resources and love, and filling it with that unforgettable, crystal-clear, affectionate laugh of hers that – together with her large, highly expressive green eyes – still lights up this part of the world; a part that, without doubt, the Good Lord created when he was feeling particularly generous.

Marco Magnifico

Villa Rezzola is located in Pugliola, a small village in the municipality of Lerici (La Spezia). The building dates back to the seventeenth century, but was constructed on the remains of a mediaeval military fortification; until the nineteenth century it was inhabited by the Botti, a noble Ligurian family. In 1900 it was acquired by a British couple, Helen Lavinia (1868–1946) and William Percy Cochrane (1860–1937), who gave the villa and the garden the appearance that it has, for the most part, today. Above all, the interiors reflect the history and life of the final owners: Countess Mara Braida Carnevale, who bought the house in 1935, and her daughter Maria Adele (1922–2020), known as Pupa, who lived in it until 2020, leaving the property to FAI in her will.

The Cochranes moved to Liguria in the early twentieth century, drawn there by the mild climate and the charms of the landscape. The impassable, sheer, almost wild cliffs of this tract of coast, which evoke the image of Romanticism, had attracted numerous foreigners since the days of the Grand Tour and, particularly in the nineteenth century, a sort of collective falling-in-love had led a large international community of intellectuals and artists to settle in the area, including Lord Byron and Percy Bysshe Shelley, who frequented Villa Rezzola with his wife, the novelist Mary Shelley. Therefore, the wide bay that embraces the entire panorama visible from the villa's terrace was in 1910 given the moniker "Gulf of Poets".

Having acquired Villa Rezzola, the Cochranes decided to undertake major works to modernise the home and the garden in keeping with the typical taste of English residences. They were responsible, for example, for the Library with the wood panelling and the typical bow window projecting outwards, the Dining Room with the ceiling decorated with neo-Gothic motifs – which are also found in the stained glass at the entrance – and the large panoramic terrace that is accessed from the Living Room. Helen Lavinia, who hailed from the countryside around Bath, could express her passion for open spaces and nature by lavishing great care on the garden of Villa Rezzola, portrayed by her in a series of watercolours, and organised – in terms of the spaces and the selection of trees and plants, as

well as the systems for irrigation – with typically British practicality.
In 1935, ownership passed to Mara Braida Carnevale, a fascinating, highly intelligent woman: the villa retains her elegant evening dresses and some of her portraits by the painter Clemente Tafuri (1903–1971). Raised in a family of conservative industrialists from the Veneto, she married Lieutenant Carlo Carnevale. She was the leading light, between Rome and Lerici, of a circle of high-calibre figures on the national and international cultural, financial and political scenes – so much so that, in 1938, she met Hitler, and in 1931, Gandhi, who gifted her a symbolic spindle that is still to be seen in the villa. She was a friend of Admiral Aimone of Savoia Aosta, a member of the Italian royal family, who resided at Villa Rezzola, which was requisitioned by the Italian government to house the High Naval Command of the Upper Tyrrhenian between 1941 and 8 September 1943. After this date, the villa was occupied by the German army, who set up a command here, with the home serving as the seat and residence of the naval captain, Rudolf Jacobs, who went down in history for having thrown off his military uniform and joined the Ligurian partisans, dying in battle in 1944 on the upland of Sarzana.

Few traces remain, aside from documentary evidence, of this absorbing chapter of the history of Villa Rezzola, which today contains a wealth of furnishings and mementos of Mara's daughter, Maria Adele Carnevale and her husband, Lieutenant Piero Miniati. In the nineteenth-century Lounge, with its stuccoed ceiling and traditionally Ligurian multicoloured mosaic stone floor, there are artefacts collected on the couple's numerous travels, including to Goa in India, with colonial furnishings, statues of Buddha and oriental ceramics.

The villa is immersed within extensive grounds. On one side, there is the formal Italian garden, with a large lawn furrowed by a ramp, and flowerbeds bordered with box hedging and vases of flowers, at the end of which, under a little pergola, Pupa Carnevale and her husband are buried. On an upper level, there is a pergola with 56 pink stone pilasters, from which abundant wisteria falls in the spring, on either side of which there are vegetable gardens, orchards and a rose garden, irrigated by channels and underground cisterns that collect rainwater and feed fountains hidden among the bamboo and lily ponds. Close by, there is a large greenhouse, in addition to a shade canopy and a seedbed for the cultivation of seeds and root cuttings: measures that betray the passion and skills of the owners in taking care of the garden, from the Cochranes right through to the last owner, who herself was passionate about botany and gardening. At the base of the villa, on the slope, stretching down almost to sea level, there is an English-style park with a dense array of holm oaks, laurels, olive trees and other Mediterranean species, amid which paths, ramps and staircases meander.

The considerable scale of the grounds can be discerned from the panoramic terrace of the Lounge, and from the terraced garden below, overlooked by a portico on the basement floor of the villa, which itself is bordered by wisteria. The most surprising vista, however, is afforded by the belvedere tower that, through the evocative arched apertures on all sides, allows the eye to take in the entire gulf of La Spezia, from Lerici to the islands of Palmaria and Tino, all the way to the town of Portovenere.

Torre e Casa Campatelli

San Gimignano, Siena

Bequest
Lydia Campatelli
2005

Guido Peyron, Lydia's uncle, with some of his paintings now on display at Torre and Casa Campatelli

I leave to FAI – Fondo per l'Ambiente Italiano the building I own in San Gimignano, complete with everything that it contains [...] and all the paintings by my uncle Guido Peyron will be included in my bequest to FAI. This bequest is subject to the following precise conditions:

– that the building shall be open to the public [...]
– that in a room on the first floor all of the paintings by G. Peyron, my mother's brother, will be put on display; the room shall be called the "G. Peyron Room"
– that the building and the tower shall be left as they are

I wish to leave my beloved house to FAI because I want those visiting San Gimignano to see what a town it is, to understand its history and to learn all about the wonders that it has to offer.

Lydia Campatelli

Lydia Campatelli

San Gimignano is a perfectly preserved mediaeval village that was recognised in 1990 as a UNESCO World Heritage Site. It is renowned for its cityscape of fourteenth-century towers, which at one time numbered 72, of which fourteen remain today. These were constructed as symbols of the power of the local families. The tower of Casa Campatelli is one of those that remain: a typical house-tower after the twelfth-century Pisan model, it was originally 11 metres tall before being raised to 28. Today it is empty, but at one time it had been a proper home, with the rooms distributed vertically on wooden floors (today partially reconstructed). Over the centuries, various buildings were added to the side of the tower to create a palazzo that, in the early nineteenth century, was acquired by the Campatelli family of Florentine entrepreneurs and landowners, with interests in the area around San Gimignano. The tower thus ended up being englobed, as it remains today, in the house of a typical upper-middle-class Tuscan family, which the last owner, Lydia Campatelli (1925–2005), wanted to donate to FAI so that it would be restored, conserved and opened up to the public.

The entrance, which at one time accommodated the farm trucks ready to unload their produce into the storage rooms below, today leads to a noble vaulted entrance hall. On the ground floor of the building, facing out over the street are three shop units, which were also donated to FAI to guarantee a financial "endowment" to support the maintenance and management of the site. At the back, the main staircase, decorated with antique prints, affords access to the *piano nobile*. The family apartment has been embellished by FAI with furniture, paintings and artefacts, some original, which were in part sourced as a result of prolonged, in-depth research into family and historical documents, carried out with a view to reinstating the appearance and atmosphere that the house must have had in the late nineteenth century, reflecting the taste favoured by the limited circle of families of the Tuscan *haute bourgeoisie*.

Welcoming guests into the main Lounge, with its beamed ceiling and *cotto*-tiled floor, is a large, neo-Renaissance fireplace with the family's coat of arms, and a group of seventeenth-century portraits, based on the model provided by the works of the Flemish artist Justus Sustermans and depicting the Grand Dukes of Tuscany. The small Lounge, in contrast, is suited to private meetings and family activities. It is full of small paintings and personal items, from family photographs to sheet music for piano, as well as embroidery and a collection of illustrated postcards.

The room coincides with the mediaeval tower, though it has lost all trace of its antecedent, with the walls painted in faux wallpaper, reapplied during the restorations thanks to fragments conserved under the plasterwork. There then follow the Study, with books and papers salvaged from the archive of the Campatelli, a Bedroom (the master, complete with alcove, is located adjacent to the main Lounge), a small Chapel, where every year a celebration is held in memory of the donor, and the Dining Room. This room, which looks onto a gallery affording a wonderful view of the countryside of San Gimignano, stands out not so much for its nineteenth-century furnishings, its chandelier or its decorated fireplace, as for its small but valuable collection, hung on the walls, of works – still lifes, landscapes, nudes and portraits – by the Florentine painter Guido Peyron (1898–1960), Lydia Campatelli's maternal uncle. Creative and inspired, an aficionado of art and automobiles, literature and cooking (he wrote the 1956 recipe book *Note sulla cucina e altre cose*, on display here), he was a friend of writers, poets and intellectuals such as Aldo Palazzeschi and Eugenio Montale, who even dedicated a poem, *Il gallo cedrone (The Capercaillie)*, to him. The attic floor provides access to the mediaeval tower, the only one in San Gimignano that has not been subject to later building work and is, therefore, visible in its original integrity. The same floor plays host to a video-installation with immersive projections featuring a fascinating account of the history of the *Torre e Casa Campatelli* (Campatelli Tower-House) and, above all, of its context: from the *borgo* of San Gimignano to the Tuscan countryside.

Orto sul Colle dell'Infinito

Recanati, Macerata

Loaned by Recanati City Council,
the Centro Nazionale di Studi Leopardiani
and the Centro Mondiale della Poesia
e della Cultura "Giacomo Leopardi"
2017

Idillio

L'Infinito

Sempre caro mi fu quest'ermo colle,
E questa siepe, che da tanta parte
Del ~~celeste confine~~ l'ultimo orizzonte il guardo esclude.
Ma sedendo e mirando, ~~un infinito~~ interminato
Spazio di là da quella, e sovrumani
Silenzi, e profondissima quiete
Io ~~mi~~ nel pensier mi fingo, ove per poco
Il cor non si spaura. E come il vento
Odo stormir ~~fra~~ tra queste piante, io quello
Infinito silenzio a questa voce
Vo comparando: ~~e~~ E mi sovvien l'eterno,
E le morte stagioni, e la presente
E viva, e 'l suon di lei. Così ~~fra~~ tra questa
~~Immensitade il mio~~ Infinità s'annega il pensier ~~si annega~~ mio:
E 'l naufragar m'è dolce in questo mare.

One of the most difficult challenges we have ever faced has been to take Giacomo Leopardi's *Infinity* – surely amongst the most beloved, well-known and often-quoted poems in Italy – and try to convince people that the title does not refer to that landscape which extends as far as the eye can see, from the end of the garden out to the horizon; rather, it refers to that inner dimension that each of us should seek and be able to recognise. This is a worthy undertaking for FAI, one that is geared towards enabling everybody, from the most refined intellectual all the way to those most resistant to reflection and to the humanities, to find something of interest in the poem; and it is very much worth doing specifically in that garden – which the young Leopardi would visit to find the silence and solitude he needed to lose himself, happily, in this state of mind – in order to give everyone access to a similar experience. The poem endeavoured to produce a sort of X-ray of this idyll, doing so with an apparent simplicity actually based on the strictest of rules. It is a poem infused with a "spirit of geometry", as the greatest living Leopardi scholar Luigi Blasucci explained to us as he led Daniela Bruno and me through this adventure full of pitfalls, after welcoming us to the austere lecture halls of the Scuola Normale Superiore in Pisa. This amounted to perhaps the greatest challenge ever taken on by FAI: to put together a guided tour of a poem, and the most famous Italian poem of all at that.

A series of fortunate coincidences made possible by the ever-inventive determination of Alessandra Stipa; a series of fortunate meetings with people who then became friends; a prestigious organisation, the National Centre for Leopardi Studies, where alongside the director Fabio Corvatta we designed a route, with input from Recanati town council and Casa Leopardi, that would help the public learn a great deal more about the unparalleled Italian genius who wrote the poem – all of these elements came together to ensure that the abandoned garden could blossom once again, enchanting visitors by taking them by the hand through the silence of a simple, monastic, natural environment, to rediscover something of themselves amid their difficult, distracted, deafening, twenty-first-century lives.

Marco Magnifico

Marco Magnifico

The manuscript of L'Infinito *by Leopardi*

The *Orto sul Colle dell'Infinito* (Garden on the Hill of Infinity) is located on the edge of the historic town of Recanati, on the high ground that, since 1837, has been named after one of the most celebrated poems in Italian literature, *Infinity* by Giacomo Leopardi (1798–1837). Enclosed within the sixteenth-century Convent of Santo Stefano and the walls that surround the town, which here are tall, potent bastions, the *orto* is a hanging garden with an extraordinary view over the rolling hills of the Marche, from the Sibillini mountains to the sea. Dotted with flowers, vegetables and fruit trees, for centuries it was a *hortus conclusus*, the typical kitchen garden of a convent, a place of silence and prayer, cultivated to meet the limited needs of the community of nuns who lived here and who looked after it until the early twentieth century.

For ten years from 1810, following the repression of the religious orders imposed by Napoleon Bonaparte, the garden was closed and abandoned. It was in this very period that the young Leopardi would often visit it, in search of a corner of peace and solitude just a stone's throw from the house where he had been born, *Casa Leopardi*, which retains the library in which he studied, created by his father Monaldo; it was right here, in 1819, that the poet conceived and set his most famous poem, *Infinity*, which describes an experience he had in this very place: the experience of the infinite.

Foto storiche del CNSL
1960
La facciata del CNSL su Via Monte Tabor

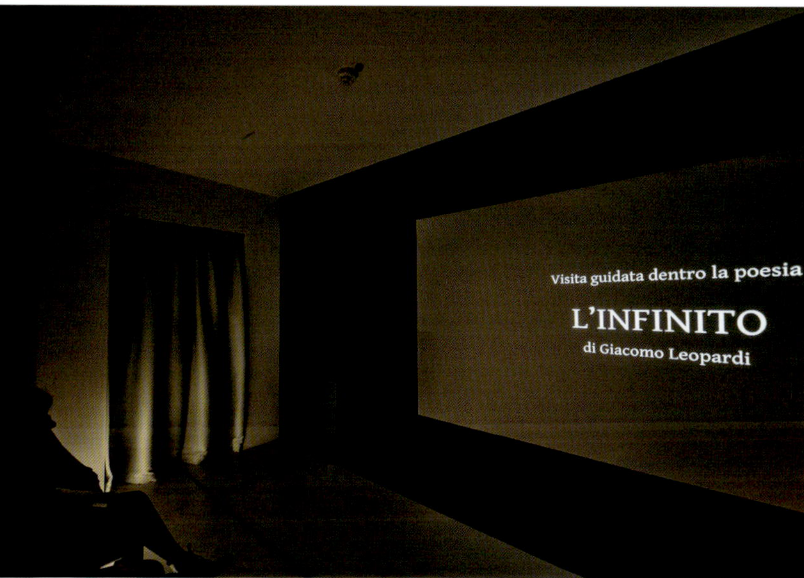

In 2019, in the poem's bicentenary year, FAI, Recanati local council, the Centro Nazionale di Studi Leopardiani (National Centre for Leopardi Studies) and the Centro mondiale della poesia (World Poetry Centre) inaugurated – in the presence of Italian President Sergio Mattarella – the reopening of the Orto sul Colle dell'Infinito. The garden, owned by the local council and entrusted to FAI, has been salvaged, with restoration of the surrounding masonry, the portico and the little chapel of the ancient convent, while new species have been planted. Today, it has achieved a sense of simplicity, as a place of tranquillity and reflection, infused with the spirituality bound up with the experience that Leopardi had here, before describing in verse his vision of infinity.

To guide the public in the footsteps of the poet, and to allow them to grasp the meaning and value of the poem, FAI has created an additional space for visitors in preparation for their visit to the garden, sited in the nearby National Centre for Leopardi Studies and run in partnership with it. In 1937, on the occasion of the centenary of the poet's death, this impressive building in the rationalist style was built between the Garden and Casa Leopardi, designed by the architect Guglielmo de Angelis d'Ossat (1907–1992) right down to the smallest details, including the high-quality furnishings and decorations, which have been conserved intact, from the Venini wall lights to the furniture made by Maggini, a local craft manufacturer. The building was conceived as a centre for studies on Leopardi and his work, with the objective of promoting an in-depth understanding of the poet on the part of scholars and enthusiasts, in part through a themed library – the only one of its type in the world – housing around 12,000 volumes, including a copy of the first printed edition of *Infinity*, published in Naples in 1835.

The Garden is accessed through the Centre, in the basement of which FAI has put together an innovative multimedia "guided tour inside *Infinity*": a video-story that, by means of immersive screenings and a narration based on the poet's own words taken from the *Zibaldone*, leads visitors on a deep re-reading of the poem, covering everything from its genesis to its editing, from its meaning to its form, thus introducing them to the experience of visiting the Garden armed with the necessary awareness to realise the value of this special place.

Bosco di San Francesco

Assisi, Perugia

Purchased thanks to a donation by
Intesa Sanpaolo
2008

A view of the extraordinary Assisan landscape in the sunset.
To the right, the silhouette of the Basilica and Monastery of Saint Francis, while the austere mass of the Rocca Maggiore stands out to the left against the summit of the hill of Assisi.

The Bosco di San Francesco in Assisi, which extends across 64 hectares, was donated by Intesa Sanpaolo to FAI on 29 October 2008, and was then opened to the public on 11 November 2011, following the completion of a project that resulted in the reinstatement of the area's original identity.

The overhaul, which involved the restoration of the fourteenth-century tower and the renovation of the paths and the ancient dry-stone walls, now allows the visitor to savour a walk through a tract of hilly Umbrian countryside – rich in olive groves, oak and holm oak, fruit trees, broom and hawthorn – leading to the Piazza della Basilica Superiore in Assisi.

It is a route that, for the visitor, also affords the opportunity for a spiritual journey, since the landscape is imbued with that sense of harmony between Man and Nature that is encapsulated by the teachings of St Francis and that also provides the backdrop for the work of Giotto.

This place, so normal and yet so special, is very much in synch with Michelangelo Pistoletto's work of land art entitled *Terzo Paradiso*, which is composed of 121 olive trees, laid out in two rows, at the centre of which there is a 12-metre pole that symbolises the union of earth and heaven.

To those who come to Assisi to admire the Basilica, Giotto's frescoes and the church of Santa Chiara, the Bosco di San Francesco offers a sort of pilgrimage through the natural world, amidst clearings and silences that invite visitors to be swept away by the beauty and sweetness of the place.

The restoration of this extraordinary environment is also symbolically significant, since the renovated landscape stands as a model of respectful use and safeguarding of the countryside, which is one of Italy's truly priceless assets.

The partnership between Intesa Sanpaolo and FAI, which has been ongoing for several years now and which has been renewed once again on this occasion, responds to the constant requirement to make the most of the beauty of the Italian landscape and to make everyone aware of the importance and uniqueness of Italy's cultural and environmental heritage.

*Giovanni Bazoli**

* Chairman of the Intesa Sanpaolo Supervisory Board at the time of donation

Near the Basilica di San Francesco, in the wall that surrounds the square, there is a large doorway. Passing through it, we leave behind the mediaeval alleyways of the old town as we enter the other half of Assisi: the *Bosco di San Francesco* (St Francis' Wood). The property encompasses 64 hectares of hillside and valley floor, where thick forests of downy oak, hornbeam and holm oak alternate with the Umbrian countryside, characterised by its typical olive groves, amid shaded paths and sun-drenched clearings, along with a mill, a mediaeval tower and the remains of an ancient convent with a thirteenth-century church.
The woodland was donated to FAI by Intesa Sanpaolo in 2008: at that time it was abandoned, wild, closed to the public and threatened by degradation and speculative development. FAI salvaged the historic landscape, restored the buildings and improved the paths, and also began to take care of the woodland, cultivating and maintaining it. In doing so, FAI has enhanced the spirit of the site, which evokes the vision of St Francis, whereby nature is a place for meditation and prayer, but also that of St Benedict, whereby it is a source of sustenance, and as such should be tamed.

In 1228, Brother Elia, the former vicar general of the monastery of San Francesco, received as a gift the plot of land identified as the Colle dell'Inferno (Hill of Hell) to be used for the construction of a Basilica to serve as the Saint's burial place. The next year a certain Monaldo di Leonardo also gave the Franciscans a wooded plot and a forest given over to the felling of timber, which stretched across the slopes of the hill, with an ancient bridge that crossed the Tescio stream: the Bosco di San Francesco.

In the mid-thirteenth century, a Benedictine nun convent was built, complete with a hospital, church, bridge and mill: this is the Santa Croce complex, a hospice where the nuns looked after the poor, elderly and unwell, offering material and spiritual assistance, while they dedicated themselves to prayer and hard work, in accordance with the Rule of St Benedict.
What remains of the convent, restored by FAI, is now home to the reception and public services area; in the mill, which remained in use until the end of the twentieth century, there is now a delightful bar.

The church of Santa Croce is part of the convent complex: it is a little chapel, intended to serve a small country congregation. The church is built in the Romanesque style, with a nave and a gabled facade, but it was overhauled in the seventeenth century following the collapse of the apsidal wall. A number of traces indicate that the interiors, today in exposed brick, were at one time plastered and probably frescoed. The fresco above the altar, *Saint Helen and the Virgin in Adoration of the Bare Cross*, is dated 1643 and attributed to the Assisan painter Girolamo Marinelli.

Another type of spirituality – secular and contemporary – finds its open-air sanctuary in a clearing on the valley floor, where in 2010 the artist Michelangelo Pistoletto created one of his celebrated works of land art, entitled *Terzo Paradiso* (Third Paradise). Having traced a furrow with a plough drawn by oxen, he then planted inside it twenty-one olive trees, which are both a fixture of the Umbrian landscape and a symbol of peace. The arrangement of the olive trees – in two rows, between which we can wander as if undergoing a ritual experience – reproduces the mathematical symbol for infinity, enriched in the centre by a third circle, which for the artist represents the ideal of a new world based on the pacific and sympathetic co-existence of mankind and nature.

Parco Villa Gregoriana

Tivoli, Roma

Concession
by State Property Agency
2002

Luigi Spaventa, the great economist, had a house in Tivoli and was involved by Vittorio Ripa di Meana – for many years Regional President of FAI Lazio – in the Roman activities of our foundation.

From his garden he had watched for years, impotent despite reminders sent to those who should have taken care of it, to the progressive, unstoppable and tragic degradation in which, after the years before, the Villa Gregoriana, a monument of European romanticism created in 1832 by Pope Gregory XVI on the ruins of a catastrophic flooding of the river Aniene, had fallen into.

Sofia Bosco, director of the FAI Office in Rome, and I, after much insistence from Professor Spaventa, went to Tivoli and, along abandoned paths, overcoming collapsing walls, landslides, festering vegetation and rubbish of all kinds (even toilets, as well as washing machines, bicycles and whatnot…) and breathing the miasma of the sewers that flowed opaquely where His Holiness had channelled the frothy waters of the Aniene, we descended to the Grotto of Neptune where in an infernal vortex the rocks shaped by years of rushing waters create an atmosphere worthy of the Styx.

The work of restoring such a vast and complex romantic landscape of steep paths carved in the rock, centuries-old vegetation plagued by long neglect, Roman ruins assailed by vegetation that favoured small collapses and topped off by the repugnant company of sewage water flowing everywhere, a terrifying but new challenge appeared to us; we were conquered; and with us all the reckless and daring FAI! For a few months we were bounced like tennis balls from one state property office to another where astonished clerks could not understand why we so ardently wanted to take care of such ruin. The handover to FAI took place during a memorable press conference that then Prime Minister Silvio Berlusconi wanted to hold at Palazzo Chigi; the duet with FAI President Giulia Maria Crespi was theatrical and delighted the dozens of journalists who attended the meeting. The four years of lengthy and highly problematic restoration work (the bottom of the villa can only be reached on foot and the helicopter cannot enter the narrow and gloomy natural gorge it contains) ended with a triumphal inauguration attended, in a jubilant Tivoli, by the President of the Republic Carlo Azeglio Ciampi accompanied by his unforgettable wife.

Marco Magnifico

"What beauty of that fair site, before art touched it! Nowhere has Nature indulged herself so freely."
This is how the Latin poet Statius (c. 45 AD – c. 96 AD) described the place in which the Parco Villa Gregoriana is today located, chosen at that time by the Roman consul Manlius Vopiscus for a luxurious, extraordinary villa of leisure in the countryside, almost suspended over the river Aniene that crossed the ancient *Tibur* (Tiber) and until the nineteenth century came crashing down in a waterfall and the end of this valley. Little is left now of the Roman villa, but the landscape is still overlooked by the two temples of the acropolis, which are almost intact, and of which one is attributed to Tiburnus, the town's eponymous hero, alongside a round temple that is very recognisable since it has been depicted by hundreds of travellers and artists.
From the eighteenth century onwards, Tivoli was one of the most popular stop-offs on the Grand Tour, and the area of what is now the FAI property was especially fascinating for writers and painters, due to its lush appearance and the powerful natural forces it embodied, and to its remaining traces of antiquity. Visitors included Chateaubriand, Turner, Corot and Ingres, amongst many others. On his trip to Italy, which lasted from 1786 to 1788, Johann Wolfgang von Goethe (1749–1832) wrote of this place that "the whole complex of the landscape with its details, its views, its waterfalls is one of those experiences which permanently enrich one's life".

During the night of 16 November 1826, a devastating flood destroyed the part of the town of Tivoli sited at the top of the valley. To deal with the disaster and prevent further flooding, the papal government, under the papacy of Gregory XVI (1765–1846), held an international competition: Clemente Folchi (1780–1868), an engineer and hydraulics expert for the Sacra Consulta, who had previously worked on the Marmore Falls, envisaged the deviating of the river towards two parallel tunnels carved into Mount Catillus in order to mitigate the raging torrent. Between 1832 and 1835, two hundred labourers used pickaxes to hollow out the 280 metre-long Gregorian Tunnels, from which to this day the new (artificially enlarged) Grand Waterfall gushes forth; at 120 metres, it is the second-highest in Italy, with only the Marmore Falls being higher. This project gave rise to the modern-day Villa Gregoriana, named after Pope Gregory XVI.

The Villa was inaugurated on 7 October 1835. On that day, visitors marvelled not only at the feat of hydraulic engineering but also, for the first time, at the new layout of the entire surrounding area, which was transformed into a public park with a great variety of trees and plants, arranged with "spontaneous naturalness" but in fact the result of a precise design. Between woodlands and clearings, caves and tunnels, waterfalls and ruins, there are paths and flights of steps that offer up perspectives on what looks like a wilderness, in line with the criteria of the Romantic garden. In a steep descent towards the "Valley of Hell", one enters the subsoil: the geological form of the site, based on tufa limestone and soft sedimentary materials, enabled the Aniene to mould and carve out karst caves, and the underground paths of the river gave rise to springs and sinkholes, such as the Grotto of Neptune and the Grotto of the Sirens, which can be visited today. To facilitate movement along the slopes, routes were laid out, including the tunnel known as the *Traforetto*, created by Napoleon's governor of Rome, General Miollis (1759–1828).

Since 2002, on the basis of a concession from the Italian State Property Agency, FAI has been taking care of Villa Gregoriana, which after a glorious past in the latter stages of its life had been abandoned, closed to the public and almost treated as a dumping ground. The caves, slopes and paths have been cleared, bringing back to light their natural conformation, the historical testimonies and the nineteenth-century landscaping. A programme of scheduled maintenance – particularly complex for a site such as this – guarantees its conservation and utilisation.

Baia di Ieranto

Massa Lubrense, Napoli

Donation Italsider
1987

Punta Campanella (centre) and the Montalto promontory (right) enclose the Bay of Ieranto. The southernmost point of the peninsula of Sorrento, Punta Campanella marks the division between the Sorrentine and the Amalfi coasts.

The donation to FAI of Ieranto Bay was the result of a very simple consideration concerning the relationship between industry and the environment.

There was a quarry there that had been used by a business for a few generations. Its purpose was now finished and I considered it our duty to restore the place to the public.

The fact that it was a place of particular beauty made the idea more interesting, but this did little to solve the general problem that had been worrying me for some time – that of handing back to the public properties that had been used by industry, in such a way as to restrict as far as possible the conflict between their economic exploitation and their enjoyment by the community.

This may appear elementary, but anyone viewing our countryside from the air sees at once that wounds inflicted by past industry are never allowed to heal, even when this can be done at little cost.

It also seemed to me that large-scale industries should feel more responsibility than others for the preservation of such unique examples of collective heritage as Ieranto. I must add that when I look around I see many other similar cases, and for this reason I hope my idea will prove contagious.

*Romano Prodi**

Romano Prodi

* President of IRI in 1987

From the village of Nerano, in the province of Naples, via a challenging path bordered by broom, myrtle and rosemary, we come to Ieranto Bay, a natural inlet spanning 47 hectares that offers a unique view of the sea stacks of Capri. Inhabited as early as the final phase of the Palaeolithic period, it was referred to by the historian and geographer Strabo (first century BC) as the site of two important temples: that of Athena and that of the Sirens. For Pliny the Elder (23–79 AD), this was the dwelling place of the mythical sea creatures encountered by Ulysses on his voyage.

Over the centuries, numerous man-made changes have visibly influenced the bay, giving rise to an unusual landscape, which is the fruit of carefully planned agricultural biodiversity combined with traditional techniques. In the early twentieth century, quarrying operations began in the bay in order to meet the increasing demand from industry and for the construction of major ports around the country. The Sorrentine peninsula constituted the ideal logistical base, both for the quality of the stone and for its location, which is easy to reach by sea. In 1910, ILVA initiated the process of purchasing the quarry and the land of the bay, and a few years later, in 1914, the first buildings were constructed, including the payroll office, the accommodation, the compressor room and the old loading bay. The population of the mining village began to swell: the local bricklayers and metalworkers were joined by more expert miners from the quarries of Sulcis and Arbatax, who created the "miners' ladder" to facilitate access to the quarries located at sea level. By 1952, the iron and steel operations began to tail off, and in 1954 the Ieranto quarry was closed for good.

In 1986, the area was donated to FAI by Italsider – which until 1945 had been involved in quarrying there – so that it could be given back to the community and not be at risk of property speculation. FAI thus began its first landscape restoration project, restoring the sixteenth-century Montalto Tower, renovating the mining village and reinstating the terrace for the cultivation of olive trees and the original Mediterranean scrub. A philological restoration was undertaken of the "cupola house", with the reconstruction of the roofs using volcanic fragments: a traditional technique rediscovered thanks to FAI.

In Ieranto, as throughout the Sorrentine peninsula, a characteristic pergola of chestnut poles and *pagliarelle* netting protects the citrus trees against night-time frosts, heavy rain and hail. The netting, made using two layers of wheat straw, is placed over the pergola in November and removed in April; after the first winter, the straw is not brought back down to the ground but stacked away up high, forming unusual sloping structures reminiscent of tents. The olive-oil mill situated within the farmhouse retains the ancient press for the crushing of olives: a process carried out with traditional techniques using materials sourced on site.

The bay's complex system of terracing is buttressed by dry-stone walls, fully restored by FAI, which are a crucial element in protecting the soil and preventing landslides. Due to the harmonious relationship between people and nature that it embodies, in 2018 UNESCO recognised the technique of these dry-stone walls as an artform in itself, adding it to the list of intangible cultural heritage.

Owing to an uneven geomorphological structure that permits the phenomenon of thermal and vegetational inversion, Ieranto's specific microclimate favours the presence of numerous native species, both animal and vegetable. The flora includes oak, maritime pine, holm oak and carob tree, but also undergrowth of cyclamen and wild asparagus. Off the coast there are immense prairies of Neptune grass (*Posidonia oceanica*), one of the most highly protected marine environments in the Mediterranean.

Thanks to FAI, in the quarry, which had been abandoned half a century before, work was done to safeguard the spontaneous recolonisation of the native flora, including rare species at risk of extinction.

The bay is located along the main migration routes of numerous species of birds, including the peregrine falcon, which nests on the imposing rocks of Mount San Costanzo. The particular nature of the environment and landscape here is formally recognised: the inland territory is part of a Site of Community Importance and is also a Special Protection Area, whereas the tract of sea across from the bay is part of the Marine Protected Area of Punta Campanella.

Casa Noha

Matera

Donation
Fodale and Latorre Families
2004

Carlo Levi, Lucania '61, *first of six assembled panels, 1961, oil on canvas, Matera, Palazzo Lanfranchi*

The memories of my visit to Casa Fodale a dozen or so years ago – maybe even more – are like a crystal-clear black-and-white photograph… The building – one of those that are all identical, simply and respectably rationalist, erected thanks to the special law of 1952 – was grey and dilapidated; the narrow, rather sad staircase led me to the modest but clean and tidy apartment. Carmelo Giovanni Fodale opened the door to me and with courteous, wordless refinement ushered me into the lounge where his sister Maria Consilia – like him, in her nineties – asked me to sit down beside her on a tasteful, late-nineteenth-century sofa. I also remember a large, elegant oleographic picture hanging above a tallboy, but most of all I was struck immediately by the style in which the two elderly siblings welcomed me and talked to me. Using just a few serene, decisive words they told me with great and surprising ease that they – along with their numerous Latorre cousins – had opted for FAI's proposal rather than the enticing offer to sell the four rooms in the Noha building that had always belonged to the family. In their now-distant memories, they described the story of their childhood and their antecedents; they would ideally have wanted some day to describe the extraordinary and at times terrible history of their town. In any case, they had decided that FAI's proposal was right for them. They remained quiet as they awaited the inevitable thanks I gave them, moved as I was and conscious of wanting to channel the gratitude of all those who would soon and in the future become aware of the gesture they had made and had communicated with such unaffected, polite decisiveness. Maria Consilia thanked me in turn with a few exquisite words accompanied by a sincere, restrained smile. After a little contextualisation, the curtain came down on our meeting, with Carmelo Giovanni Fodale accompanying me out into the street. I cannot forget the old-school manner in which – sending me on my way as I got into the car – he rapidly removed the hat from his head and bid me affectionately adieu with a flick of his elderly hand. I never saw them again.

Marco Magnifico

Marco Magnifico

FAI's first Property in the Basilicata region, donated in 2004 by the Fodale and Latorre families, Casa Noha is located near Matera Cathedral, at the summit of the Civita, which is the heart of the old town. The Civita is sited on a rocky spur above the Sasso Caveoso and the Sasso Barisano districts, which are natural *cavae* in the shape of an amphitheatre, formed by buildings hewn out of the rock of the Murgia plateau of Matera – located behind a deep gorge called the Gravina – which were inhabited from prehistoric times up until the second half of the twentieth century.
The constant increase of an ever-more isolated and poverty-stricken population made the Sassi the symbol of the anachronistic clash between the *modus vivendi* inherited from the past and the needs of contemporary society. It was a disconnect that would take on the dramatic aspects captured by Carlo Levi in his novel *Christ Stopped At Eboli*, in which he describes the condition of a people who, surrounded by animals at all times, struggle to stay alive in the dark horror of the caves carved out of the tufa stone within the intricate labyrinth of the Sassi, at that time still without lighting or a sewerage system. It was only in 1952 that the Special Law for Matera and the new land use plan led to the total depopulation of the Sassi, which were deemed unfit for human habitation. In late 1993, UNESCO declared the districts of the Sassi to be a World Heritage Site.
Casa Noha represents one of the most significant examples of residential architecture in this unusual geographical context.
It is composed of five simple stone rooms, embellished by cornices, barrel-vaulted ceilings and tufa inlays, within a noble palazzo dating back to the sixteenth century.
At one time, it was the residence of the de Noha family, who hailed from the Salento area. They were one of the aristocratic families who eventually died out in Matera, but prior to that, from the fifteenth century onwards, they had found in the Civita the ideal place for the construction of their homes.
The building passed from the

de Noha family to the Latorre and subsequently the Fodale.
Following a meticulous conservative restoration process, Casa Noha now provides visitors with a "gateway" to the city, thanks to an all-new, captivating multimedia project that describes the area from various perspectives, encompassing everything from architecture and art history to archaeology and the history of cinema. Indeed, for the first time, FAI has chosen to focus not on one of its Properties but on the context that surrounds it, through an innovative journey that envelopes the viewer in a uniquely immersive experience. Covering Matera's history from prehistoric times to the present day, the story-based film entitled *The Invisible Sassi: An Extraordinary Journey through the History of Matera*, directed by Giovanni Carrada in 2014 and projected onto the stone walls of the residence, offers – through its images, stories, sounds and interwoven references – the first complete reconstruction of the town's past. It includes a wealth of new, invaluable documentary material, the main objective of which is not simply to encourage tourism but to offer visitors content and tools to allow them to explore the city in a conscious, curious and profound way, fully grasping the meaning of this truly ancient place.
In 2019, the year in which Matera was named European Capital of Culture, Casa Noha inaugurated a new display geared towards telling the story of the town: an interactive multimedia table that provides an overview of the townscape and the surrounding area, recommending visits to special places, alongside themed itineraries through the quarters of the historical centre, nature trails and trips to the sets of arthouse films. A special route, put together by the Olivetti Historical Archive Association, is dedicated to the discovery of the peripheral residential districts that were constructed in the 1950s following the evacuation of the Sassi, which benefitted from the contribution of Adriano Olivetti and of a number of the leading architects of the twentieth century.

Abbazia di Santa Maria di Cerrate

Lecce

Concession by Provincia di Lecce
2012

Reproduction of the 1692 plateau depicting the "Abbadia di S. Maria a Cerrate sita nelle pertinenze della Terra di Trepuzzi"

The FAI in Cerrate is due to the stubborn insistence of lawyer Giorgio Aguglia, head of the FAI delegation in Lecce until 2011; a cultured gentleman of old, Aguglia has always been very active as a citizen, and as soon as he was appointed head of the delegation, he set about restoring dignity to the agonising Abbey of Cerrate. Property of the Province of Lecce, it had been radically and heavily restored in the 1970s by architect Franco Minissi according to the criteria of the time, while other absolutely incongruous interventions had been carried out in the 1990s. The Abbey was open for visits but in a state of neglect and desolating sloppiness. So insistent was Aguglia that one day in early spring I arrived with him at Cerrate; the blue of the sky, the monumental olive groves as far as the eye could see (now destroyed by xylella) and fields full of shy orange marigolds surrounded the church built in the eleventh century by Tancred of Hauteville and the monastic and agricultural buildings that enclose it like a treasure to be protected; the enchantment took hold of us, however, soon giving way to the despondency generated by the large damp patches that drew greenish gorges around the Byzantine frescoes, by the dark lichens that soiled and corroded the twisted and mysterious figures of the Romanesque capitals in the pilgrims' porch and by the small, dried-up historic citrus grove. What came next is the story of the entrusting of the entire complex to FAI by the Province of Lecce, followed by a lengthy restoration as passionate as it was fortunate, which led to the discovery of the rare Eucharistic stamp from the twelfth century, carefully buried when the Byzantine rite was banned by papal decree, and, more recently, to the reconstruction, in the place where it had been until the 1970s, of the Baroque altar of Our Lady, which was reconsecrated with great popular acclaim in 2018.

That day, the church of Santa Maria di Cerrate regained its soul; a church is a church and reducing it to a museum of itself had, in the second half of the last century, temporarily separated it from its millennial history; but the wound was healed.

Marco Magnifico

Marco Magnifico

The *Abbazia di Santa Maria di Cerrate* (Abbey of Santa Maria di Cerrate) was erected around the twelfth century amid the olive groves of the flat Salento countryside, in what is today known as Squinzano, in the municipality of Lecce. According to one legend, it was founded in the place where, during a hunt, the Virgin Mary appeared to King Tancred of Hauteville (c. 1138–1194), Count of Lecce. It is more likely, however, that the founding of the complex dates back to the early twelfth century, when Bohemond I of Hauteville (1058–1111), son of Robert Guiscard (1015–1085), encouraged the settlement of – and the construction of monasteries for – Greek monks, of Byzantine rite and culture, who had come from Byzantium and established themselves in this part of Italy following the persecutions of the eighth century. The abbey, the earliest extant reference to which dates from 1133, was certainly active until the fifteenth century, when it was first abandoned before being resuscitated thanks to its transfer under the control of the Hospital of the Incurables in Naples, which invested in the maintenance of the building, receiving in return the income from farming. A second period of neglect followed its documented plundering by the Turks in 1711, after which the abbey, no longer a monastery but now a typical large farm, specialised in oil production and tobacco processing.

Having been acquired by the Province of Lecce in 1965, by which time the farm was no longer operational, it was salvaged as a monument thanks to a restoration by architect Franco Minissi (1919–1996). In 2012 it was entrusted by the Province to FAI, becoming FAI's first and only Property in Puglia. Recent archaeological excavations have brought to light traces of a building dating from the eighth century, as well as signs of even earlier activity on the site, but the abbey, based on historical sources and on an analysis of the architecture and frescoes, dates from the twelfth century.

The Church of Santa Maria is a fine example of Puglian Romanesque, with a gabled facade and a central rose window, Lombard bands and half pilasters carved from the typical *pietra leccese* stonework, as is the portal, surmounted by an arch with high-reliefs reproducing scenes from the New Testament. The internal layout is also Romanesque, resembling a basilica chamber subdivided into a nave and two aisles with apses.

The internal decoration, in contrast, is entirely Byzantine, and constitutes the tangible embodiment of a fusion between Norman culture and Greek culture, the latter always having been rooted in this border territory, jutting out as it does into the Mediterranean. On the walls and under the ogival arches that separate

the nave and the aisles, there is a parade of saints, bishops and hermits painted in the typical style of Byzantine iconography of the twelfth and thirteen centuries; frescoes applied a couple of centuries later were subjected to the *strappo* (detachment) process in the 1970s – and are currently conserved in the adjacent workshop – in order to allow the older decoration to be visible. Leaning against the Church is a thirteenth-century portico, supported by twenty-four columns with stone capitals sculpted into organic and zoomorphic elements taken from mediaeval bestiaries. Scattered around the Church are the so-called Monks' House and a building dating from the early sixteenth century, presumably an old stable, between which there is a well made of *pietra leccese* dating from 1585. The Monks' House takes its name from the fact that the abbey played host to a monastic community from at least 1154, the year in which a manuscript was written that cites a certain "Paolo egumeno" (Paul the abbot) of the abbey of Cerrate. Probably dating from around the same time is a precious find that emerged from recent excavations and bears witness to the practising of the Byzantine cult: a mould sculpted and inscribed in stone, which was used to stamp the bread intended for the celebration of the Easter Eucharist in the Greek rite.

To evoke the Byzantine origins of Santa Maria di Cerrate – and underline the link with a culture that, centuries later, can still be discerned within the Salentine tradition, for instance in the linguistic enclave of *Grecìa* – FAI, which reopened the Church to worship after decades, decided to celebrate mass once a month in the Latin rite and in the Greek rite.

The frescoes at Santa Maria di Cerrate reflect Byzantine religious imagery: behind the main altar there is the Christ Pantocrator – sovereign of the universe – flanked by two angels; just below, the Virgin Mary in prayer, surrounded by the archangels Michael and Gabriel and by the apostles. Further down, at head height, there are the bishops and the deacons, who are depicted life-size and who participate almost physically in the liturgy celebrated on the altar. All of the other surfaces of the church, from the nave and the aisles to the intradoses, feature a dense, ordered multitude of saints grouped by category – warriors, medics, monks and martyrs – and of anchorites, ascetics and prophets with middle-eastern features, holding symbols and texts that tell their story: fifty or so characters, akin to a crowd, who populated the church and literally surrounded the faithful, involving them in the celebration. The ordered series of saints is thrown into disorder on the wall of an aisle, which evidently collapsed and was recomposed with the blocks in a random order, giving rise to a curious puzzle, with certain fragments very well conserved in terms of their colours and characteristics thanks to the protection afforded by a subsequent fresco, now removed.

Within the Church there are three altars: the high altar, with a ciborium dating from 1269; that in the right aisle, dedicated in 1661, after the plague, to the patron saint of Lecce, Saint Orontius; and that leaning against a column in the left aisle, with an inscription on the frieze that states it was constructed in 1642, but in place of a previous altar, destroyed by the passage of time. This latter altar, the fulcrum of authentic devotion on the part of the local community, had been dismantled in the 1970s, to bring the building back to its original, mediaeval appearance; FAI salvaged and recomposed its 26 pieces, adding a copy of the original canvas with the image of Mary – seen in photographs of the site – which was commissioned from a local painter.

Even in the twelfth century, the Abbey could count on considerable agricultural income thanks to its extensive Properties. In the nineteenth century, it still owned 250 hectares of terrain, cultivated with olive trees and cereals. Two ancient, evocative underground olive-oil mills, called *trappiti* – which still show traces of the grindstones that were turned by a mule, as well as the receptacles, the stone basins and the presses – indicate that olive oil was also produced at the Abbey, and from the nineteenth century the process was carried out in a modern workshop next to the Church, with the estate manager's house on the first floor of the building. Cereals were also ground here, and FAI has reinstated, in the room of the original mill, a rare intact example of a friction mill, which was stored in a warehouse, thus returning the artefact to its rightful place and purpose.
In a corner within the Abbey's walls, 51 orange trees of the "Portugal" type are cultivated. Outside the walls, a large plot has been set aside by FAI for an experimental project for the cultivation of olive trees that are resistant to *xylella*, the pathogenic bacterium that has previously struck and continues to threaten the olive groves that extend as far as the eye can see and are symbolic of the Salentine landscape.

Giganti della Sila e Casino Mollo

Spezzano della Sila, Cosenza

Giganti della Sila
Loaned by the Sila National Park, 2016

Casino Mollo
Donation Giovanna, Beatrice and Maria Silvia Mollo, 2016

Fallistro is a place that is very dear to us, and is closely bound up with our memories of a happy childhood; for this reason, we had always intended to protect and safeguard that rather magical, rather sacred atmosphere you can feel there. After the establishment of the park, together with Vincenzo we thought about opening the lodge up to the public, and we put together various proposals that could be financed, and then Vincenzo came up with the idea of working with FAI, and Laura Carratelli can confirm that she was asked if it would be possible for her to collaborate with us, although this was not quite the right solution… but we made a number of attempts to bring the farmhouse and the spinning mill back to life and to make the most of them. […] When the directors of the park requested the input of FAI, well, that put the idea back on the table… so that's how we ended up with the story we're telling today. Not only did we arrive at a wide-ranging agreement and a shared intention about what to do and how to go about it, we also realised that FAI could do what we wanted to do much better than we could hope to, and so for us giving the farmhouse to FAI was not about losing it, but really about gaining it for everyone, because that was really what Vincenzo had in mind, and I would like to thank everyone who helped us and supported us. We knew FAI and we knew how they worked, and so we had confidence in the people to whom we were entrusting this Property and we were sure that they would do a great job with it.

Maria Silvia Mollo

The Fallistro Nature Reserve is a woodland that forms part of the Sila National Park and extends across 5 hectares in the municipality of Spezzano della Sila (in the province of Cosenza), at an altitude of 1,400 metres. It is a wood that is small yet monumental, since it is home to 60 black pines and sycamores rising up to 45 metres of height, with trunks up to two metres wide and an average age of 350 years. These are the so-called "Giants of the Sila", a rare and precious testament to the authentic landscape of the Sila, the name of which comes from the Latin *silva*, meaning "woodland".

At the time of the Romans, this territory – naturally home to high-trunked trees – was *ager publicus*, the property of the State, which had the exclusive use of its natural resources, specifically its precious timber, which was the source of, for example, the mainmast of the ship designed by Archimedes for the tyrant of Syracuse, Hiero II, in 240 BC, the trusses of St Peter's Basilica in Rome, and the beams of the roof of the Palace of Caserta. Some of it can possibly be found even in a number of American skyscrapers: at the end of the Second World War, some of the Sila timber was given to the Allies as a token of gratitude for the Liberation.

The woodland was exploited for a great many years for the tar it could offer. The *picaro* or *piciaro* was a woodsman who specialised in slicing the bark with deep, geometric grooves that in spring would ooze an odorous resin, used for medicinal potions to combat arthritis and dog bites, but also in cosmetics, to waterproof the hulls of boats and to seal barrels and amphorae of wine. The trunks of the "Giants" were also utilised for their *teda*, a combustible material composed of resinous shards. To extract it, the trees were cut into so deeply that they ended up with cavities the size of small sheds, where the shepherds would take shelter during the transhumance.

A notarial deed from 1631 records the purchase of this portion of the estate by the Mollo, a rich and influential landowning family from Cosenza. The woodland was planted at that time to protect their hunting lodge from the freezing winter winds and to shelter the flocks. In the nineteenth century, the site also included a mill, two chapels, a stable later transformed into a spinning mill, a water tank, a greenhouse and a tower. Over time, the Mollo family established a company for the supply of timber, fodder and agricultural produce (such as wheat and potatoes), with livestock (in part for transhumant pastoralism) and a silk-spinning mill (starting with the cultivation of mulberry), which proved particularly successful: the *organzine*, *soft silk* and *setone* produced here in bales of raw yarn were sent to the main European markets in Marseilles, London and Lyon.

The company having shut down, in the 1980s the lodge went back to being a simple summer residence for the Mollo family: the final owners, sisters Maria Silvia, Giovanna and Beatrice Mollo, donated it to FAI in 2016, also in memory of their mother, Paola Manes (1920–1991), who fought courageously to defend the woodland from the threat of felling; it was thanks in part to her protests that the Fallistro Nature Reserve, safeguarded by the Sila National Park, was established in 1987.

Since 2014, the Sila National Park has been one of the biosphere reserves recognised by the Man and the Biosphere (MAB) programme, launched by UNESCO to identify and protect landscapes that have retained a harmonious balance between human activity, the natural environment and urban settlements. In the woodland of the Giants of Fallistro, the decision was taken to make the most of the work of nature: this is a Guided Biogenetic Nature Reserve, where human intervention is limited solely to helping nature to take its course, offering a wilderness to animals that now live in few other sites in Italy, such as the Calabrian black squirrel (*Sciurus meridionalis*), which is found only in the Calabria and Basilicata regions.

The Giants of Fallistro Reserve was entrusted to FAI on a concessionary basis in 2016 by the Sila National Park. The nearby Casino Mollo (Mollo Lodge), donated to FAI in the same year, is currently being restored and will become a visitor centre and hub for a cultural project geared towards illustrating and describing this special place, where nature and history come together.

Giardino della Kolymbethra e Case Montana

Valle dei Templi, Agrigento

Giardino della Kolymbethra
Concession by Regione Siciliana
1999

Case Montana
Purchased from Caterina Di Grado
2018

The beginning of the exciting story of the marriage between the Kolymbethra Garden and the FAI is due to a daring young man from Agrigento, recently graduated in agronomy; he had read about FAI in Alitalia's *Ulisse 2000* magazine and one day in 1999 he showed up in our Milan offices saying he had something very important to tell us; we were, Giuseppe Lo Pilato, known as Peppe, and I, much younger and our future was nourished by dreams; his dream was to give a future to the Kolymbethra Garden, a citrus grove that he said was magic in the heart of the Valley of the Temples, now reduced to a dump and open sewer that he wanted to bring back to life; our dream was to bring the FAI experience to Sicily, one of the most beautiful regions in the world.

The following week with Peppe we were making our way with a sickle through the brambles that had invaded the historical path between the temple of Castor and Pollux – the symbol of Agrigento – and the valley of the Kolymbethra; Peppe's dad, who was with us and had cultivated those orange trees as a young man, picked and peeled an orange tree for me with a few confident gestures; perhaps the best orange of my life. It was love at first sight.

A few weeks later Giulia Maria Crespi and Renato Bazzoni came to Agrigento; same scene, same love. The Sicilian Region was then led by Angelo Capodicasa, from Agrigento; he had faith in FAI and the Kolymbethra was entrusted to FAI with its enormous load of problems and its unrepeatable charm and with the task of erasing the long neglect and opening it to the public. Since then, with tireless work shared step by step with the Park of the Valley of the Temples, the Kolymbethra has been reborn a little every year, with its orange trees of every species, its centuries-old olive trees, the purest waters flowing from the hypogea excavated two thousand five hundred years ago and the vegetable gardens that Peppe's father began to keep like embroidery; and then, always in full agreement with the Superintendency and the Archaeological Park, excavations, restorations, discoveries, studies…

A story that in 2018 was enriched by the purchase by FAI, after almost twenty years of a close court to the owners, of the farmhouse once inhabited by the family of farmers who for generations had cultivated that garden; because in Sicily, when a citrus grove is so beautiful, it is called a garden!

Case Montana, this is the name of that little nest on the calcarenite cliff that did not collapse only because it knew that sooner or later FAI would take care of its poor structures, which are still awaiting, as I write, the delicate restoration that will bring them back to glory; a story yet to be written…

Marco Magnifico

Between the temple of Castor and Pollux and the temple of Vulcan, in the heart of the Valley of the Temples in Agrigento, there lies Kolymbethra Garden, an immense green area enclosed by massive walls of tufa limestone.

A place celebrated by literati and poets since antiquity and an unmissable stop on the Grand Tour, before becoming utterly abandoned, it was entrusted in 1999 by Sicily Region to FAI, which in November 2001, having completed a painstaking restoration, opened it to the public. Today, the landscape is an intact wonder, its historic and natural vocations reinstated, but when Kolymbethra was handed over to FAI it had a markedly different appearance: it was a dry gorge, covered in wild vegetation and full of rubbish, obstructing its lifeblood – the waterways.
According to the historian Diodorus Siculus, who lived in the first century BC, it was in 480 BC that the tyrant of Agrigento, Theron, chose this valley, wedged between the acropolis and the residential quarters, to create an artificial basin with a circumference of more than a kilometre and a depth of almost nine metres. He ordered these monumental and strategic public works in order to meet the water requirements of a city which at that time had a population of 200,000. There was no citrus grove, and in its place there was only water, channelled from the two rivers *Akragas* and *Hypsas*, held back further downstream by a dam of stone blocks and maintained at a specific level depending on the seasons – refilled or emptied when required thanks to conduits for inflow and outflow. The finest architects in fifth-century BC Agrigento designed a complicated subterranean hydraulic infrastructure, but as soon as it was no longer maintained, it ceased to function properly and the artificial basin, now buried, became a garden.
The cultivation of citrus groves was introduced in the Middle Ages, and it is still in use today. Since then, the valley has been known as a "garden", thus stressing, alongside its productiveness, the aesthetic and sensory pleasure offered by these fruits.

The five hectares of Kolymbethra Garden feature a notable variety of trees and landscapes, amounting

to a unique legacy of biodiversity. The rockiest areas play host to typical species of Mediterranean scrub, such as myrtle, mastic tree, terebinth, phillyrea, euphorbia and broom. The citrus grove is located in the flat expanse of the valley floor, beyond the small river bordered by reeds, along which willows and silver poplars grow. The grove includes lemon, mandarin and orange trees of various varieties, and is still irrigated according to the Arabian tradition. Watering is almost ritualistic, carried out on specific days at particular times, with the water being released into specially dug channels, spreading its way across those areas not protected by barriers, soaking the roots of the trees within square basins delineated by earthen ditches, in a geometric weave lacing its way across the ground, which at first sight is hard to comprehend.

In March 2005, FAI completed the salvaging and restoration of the garden's water network, reinstating the ancient waterways based on the construction of hypogea – or artificial underground tunnels – that to this day collect water deep down and thus enable the irrigation of the soil. For FAI, the opening to the public of the hypogea – the only ones that can be visited and walked along anywhere in the valley – forms part of a more general enhancement project that aims to develop Kolymbethra Garden also as an archaeological site, in addition to its value in environmental and landscape terms. The aim is to serve as an example of the active safeguarding of a traditional agrarian landscape, which encompasses productive, environmental, cultural, ethical and aesthetic functions.

In 2019, FAI acquired the ruins of two simple rustic buildings, the *Case Montana*, built right on the edge of one of the rocky crags that mark out the garden area. Built in the mid-eighteenth century and inhabited until the mid-twentieth by the farmers who worked the surrounding land, following an appropriate conservative restoration project they will house displays illustrating the long history of the garden.

Saline Conti Vecchi

Assemini, Cagliari

Conti Vecchi's property cared for by FAI
2017

Saline buildings in a 1937 photo

When illustrating to colleagues, journalists and friends our commitment to open the *Saline Conti Vecchi* (Conti Vecchi Saltworks) in Cagliari to the public, almost everyone – rather taken aback by the "novelty" that an operation of this type represented for FAI – asked me: "But are they beautiful?". With my customary frankness, I always answered by saying "I don't know!"; "What do you mean you don't know?" was always then the baffled reaction. My answer, which was not without a polemical element, arose out of my frustration towards the abuse and banalisation of the concept of beauty. When, way back in 1998, we staged at San Martino al Cimino a National Conference entitled *Beauty*: *Situation and Prospects for a Neglected Concept*, we found ourselves showered with opprobrium from a plethora of "intellectuals" who portrayed us as a bunch of "well-meaning ladies who concern themselves with beauty", despite the fact that high-profile (male) figures such as Federico Zeri, Remo Bodei and the conductor Giuseppe Sinopoli had participated. After that experience, talking about Beauty, and about the world saved by it à la Dostoyevsky, gradually – and increasingly – became a customary thing to do, and then it even became *de rigueur*, hence a certain aversion to doing so on my part… and hence also the "fun" that I get from giving a rather trenchant response. Are the Conti Vecchi Saltworks beautiful? They may be beautiful but also a little bit ugly, if you like! It depends on whether it's one of those Sardinian days with the west wind blowing, with that cobalt sky and the evaporating basins full of flamingos, the blood-red salt ponds and the mountains of blinding-white salt; or alternatively, if it's a grey day, with the salt ponds empty and lifeless… then it's a different story. But it is not always and not only "ordinary" beauty that must guide our desire to get to know a place! The Conti Vecchi Saltworks are much more than that, since they encapsulate the mutable, coarse, intense world of the marshland, they embody the history of mankind's ancient ingenuity in the use of the generous resources made available by nature, they speak of the intelligent and tireless labour of the people behind them, toiling away day in, day out, at an utterly exhausting task. Beautiful? Yes… but there's more to them than that!

Marco Magnifico

Marco Magnifico

The Saline Conti Vecchi (Conti Vecchi Saltworks) are located in the Santa Gilla lagoon, in Cagliari. It was 1919 when engineer Luigi Conti Vecchi (1850–1927) submitted the project for the reclamation of the marshy, malaria-infested area also known as the *Stagno* (Pond) of Cagliari. The ambitious, innovative plan envisaged the construction of a saltworks to reinstate a historic vocation of Sardinia and make the most of an area at the outskirts of the city, contributing to its economic and social development.
Despite opposition on the part of those who defended the traditional industry of fishing in the lagoon, in 1921 the General Committee for Reclamations gave its assent, granting the concession to create a plant in the areas of Santa Gilla owned by the Public Property Agency, to produce not only salt but also various by-products sourced from the brine, to be used by the chemical and farming industries, such as chloride, magnesium sulphate and potassium fertilisers.

In 1927, after the building of the infrastructure (embankments, canals, roads, houses, two bridges and a port), the first experimental harvest was carried out, and the following year 70,000 tonnes of salt were produced – a figure that rose rapidly to 240,000. Thus came into being the Ing. Luigi Conti Vecchi company, the arc of which reflects that of many similar industrial concerns in twentieth-century Italy: established in 1929, over the subsequent decades it provided employment for about 1,000 people. A true "salt community" grew up around the plant, with houses, schools and leisure facilities for the families of owners, directors and workers, who lived together in the village of Macchiareddu, between the saltworks and Porto San Pietro – a quay immersed in wonderful natural surroundings.

The saltworks created by Conti Vecchi were on the cutting edge and self-sufficient: in addition to the infrastructure for the cultivation and harvesting of salt, they boasted two workshops (mechanical and electrical), a carpenter's shop and a plant for forging and smelting. They were also equipped with machinery for the handling and shipping of the product, with conveyor belts capable of lifting the salt up to 15 metres and to load it onto the barges moored at the saltworks own little port.

The welfare system designed for Conti Vecchi was also state of the art, and included the provision of a shuttle between Macchiareddu and Cagliari, the organising of summer camps for the children of the village, and a constant supply of subsidised food for the inhabitants.

In the mid-twentieth century, the inevitable technological developments led to the mechanisation of production, the elimination of certain processes and the depopulation of the workers' village; with the restructuring came the first sackings, and employee numbers decreased yet further. In 2017, Conti Vecchi, in agreement with FAI, launched an innovative project to illustrate the original appearance, function and context of the industrial site, and to showcase, preserve and promote the heritage – in cultural terms and in terms of the landscape – that this industrial experience represented for Sardinia and for Italy.

The rooms within the production site, which originally served as offices for the management and the administration of the saltworks, have been restored by FAI, so that the architecture, decorations, furnishings and artefacts resemble as closely as possible those in the 1930s, when the saltworks were constructed. The offices have been overhauled to include original archive material, describing the history, the places and the people who lived and worked here, offering a very particular experience of "time travel".

Two immersive screenings today enrich the visitor experience: in the mechanical engineering workshop, the video *A misura di Sardegna* (Scaled for Sardinia) charts the history of the far-sighted business created by Luigi Conti Vecchi and of the industrial development of the island from the early nineteenth century to the present day, whereas in the former carpenter's shop the evocative film *Un anno nella Salina* (A Year in the Saltworks) focuses on the landscape of the lagoon and the current operations of the plant, whereby the production of salt – today, as yesterday – is entrusted to the sun, the sea and the wind, the cycles of the seasons and, more generally, the rhythms of nature.

The saltworks are divided into two large areas: 1,900 hectares of evaporating basins, where the salt is gradually concentrated, and 273 hectares of salt ponds, where the salt sinks and accumulates on the bottom.

The evaporating basins have colours that range from navy blue to the sky blue of the sea. In the salt ponds, in contrast, as the salt builds up the water starts to turn first pink and then an intense red: this phenomenon is due to the presence of *Dunaliella salina*, a microscopic algae rich in beta-carotene that represents the first link in the food chain on which the *Artemia salina* – a brine shrimp measuring around 5 mm – depends, as do the flamingos. It is thanks to the micro-algae, absorbed by feeding on the brine shrimp, that the adult flamingos acquire the typical pink colouration of their plumage.

The salt production cycle gets under way in March, when the sea water is collected via a draining pump and channelled towards the basins, where it begins to evaporate as its salinity gradually starts to rise. In May, it is taken to the highest point of the saltworks – 11 metres above sea level – and, by means of gravity, is distributed into the salt ponds. Thanks to the summer temperatures and the dry north-westerly wind, the water evaporates almost entirely and the salt drops to the bottom, where by the end of the summer a layer of 15-20 cm of sodium chloride has accumulated.

From September, the harvesting begins in earnest, salt pond by salt pond: the salt, arranged into long piles, is loaded onto trucks and taken to the collection areas, where the conveyor belts enable the amassing of two white mountains, which serve as open-air storage depots for the salt in the run-up to being sold.

Due to the rich ecosystem of the area, and especially of the evaporating basins, the Pond of Cagliari is one of the 53 Italian sites recognised as being "of international importance: by the Ramsar (Iran) Convention on Wetlands, an intergovernmental treaty stipulated in 1971 for the conservation and rational use of wetlands and their resources. The Ramsar status has since been complemented by the statuses of Special Protection Area, Site of Community Importance and Important Bird Area; indeed, the lagoon is home to 35,000 birds of around forty different species, including herons, little egrets, shelducks, ducks and black-winged stilts.

Other FAI Properties

Torre di Velate

Velate, Varese

Donation
Leopoldo Zambeletti
1989

The Torre di Velate, an imposing presence, dominates the village of the same name just outside the gates of Varese, on a rise overlooking the road that leads from the town to Lake Maggiore. Erected in the eleventh century as a military outpost, the Tower was part of a long chain of defensive garrisons posted to control the roads connecting the Po Valley to the rest of northern Italy. Specifically, the road between Milan and Switzerland, often used by merchants, passes through the valley nearby. In the twelfth century, during the wars between Milan and Como, the Tower was semi-destroyed and lost its original function. The massive 33-metre-high square lost two of its sides, only one of which, made sturdier by the staircase embedded in it, remains in its entirety. The Tower, a fixture in the hilly panorama around Varese for 1,000 years, has a deeply symbolic value for residents of the area. Donated to FAI in 1989, it can be visited from the outside only.

Velarca

Tremezzina, Como

Donation
Aldo and Maria Luisa Norsa
2011

The Norsas are a family of intellectuals, who in 1958 commissioned the Milanese practice BBPR (Belgiojoso, Banfi, Peressutti and Rogers) to design a houseboat to be berthed in Tremezzina, on the western shore of Lake Como. Out of the four architects, it was Ernesto Nathan Rogers in particular who dealt with the operational aspects of the project, and who exploited the hull of the *Corriere Tremezzino*, a historic lighter, to create the Velarca, a nautical response to the Velasca Tower, the celebrated Milanese skyscraper designed by the same group. The connection between the outside and the inside of the houseboat is the high cylindrical section made from teak, with an internal staircase leading to the residential area. With great practical spirit, the architects carved out from the restricted surface area of the boat a modern and comfortable home. The bow houses the two main cabins and the lounge-cum-dining room; the kitchen and bathrooms occupy the flanks of the boat, whereas the stern features another cabin, the study and the closet. After fifty years of pleasant, floating vacations, in 2011 Aldo and Maria Luisa Norsa decided to donate the Velarca to FAI, prompted to make this generous gesture by the "exemplary way in which the Trust deals with protection" and further convinced by the nearby presence of the Villa del Balbianello and the Torre del Soccorso, which, together with the Velarca, may give rise to a new "heritage hub" in the Como area.

Torre del Soccorso
Tremezzina, Como

Bequest
Rita Emanuela Bernasconi
2010

The Torre del Soccorso rises up on a rocky spur above the village of Tremezzina, standing out against Lake Como, opposite the Comacina Island. Its imposing Moltrasio-stone walls were probably erected in the twelfth-thirteenth centuries as part of a larger defensive system that encompassed the nearby castle on Comacina Island, for which the tower provided cover, and the fortifications at Sala, Lezzeno and Cavagnola. In the twelfth century, the Tower was involved in two significant clashes that saw the island ally with Milan against the city of Como.
The Comascans destroyed the local fortifications, condemning the Torre del Soccorso to the state of neglect in which it was to languish over the following centuries. It was only in 1954 that the Tower was given a new lease of life thanks to the intervention of architect Clemente Bernasconi, who at the time was the Supervisor of Monuments for Lombardy and who purchased the entire complex in order to transform it into his family's summer residence. The property was inherited by his daughter Rita, who bequeathed it to FAI in 2011. The Foundation will thus create a link between the Tower and the nearby Villa del Balbianello.

Mulino "Maurizio Gervasoni"
Roncobello, Bergamo

Purchased from the Gervasoni Family thanks to a donation by Intesa Sanpaolo
2005

Located in the small mountain hamlet of Bàresi, in Val Brembana, the rural stone structure dates to the seventeenth century and still contains a walnut press, a flourmill (dated 1674) and traces of an old bread oven. The activities of these structures benefited dozens of communities in the Valley, who for centuries obtained their flour and bread here, as well as oil for food and for lamps. Above the entrance is the fresco *Madonna with Child*, and a walnut tree is shown on the right. Due to its historical, ethnographical and anthropological importance (the entire area, in fact, bears signs of human settlements since the Bronze Age), the Mill has been protected by the Ministry of Cultural Affairs. In addition, in 2003 it was voted the second most popular site in FAI's survey, *Places of the Heart*. FAI's plan included a restoration of the building and its mechanisms, so that the precious historical memory it contains can be preserved.

Antica edicola dei giornali

Mantova

Purchased from the Gandolfi Family thanks to a public subscription
1992

In 1882, the town council granted Ulisse Sicola, a Mantuan citizen, a permit to open a newspaper kiosk in Piazza Sant'Andrea, in the very centre of town, near the famous church designed by Leon Battista Alberti. A few decades later, in 1925, he was asked to transfer his kiosk to Piazza Canossa – where it still stands today – "so as not to interfere with the triumphal architecture of the Basilica". Built atop an octagonal cement platform, the structure has a low baseboard in iron and sheet metal supporting a sequence of neo-Gothic mullioned windows. The roof peaks in an embossed metal spire. After having obtained the protection of the competent authorities, in 1992 the Mantua FAI Delegation purchased this little gem, which was in a sorrowful state, had it restored thoroughly and re-opened it. In 2004, it was again cleaned and re-painted as part of an operation entitled "the Newsstand rediscovered", and its electrica system was brought up to code.

Castel Grumello

Montagna in Valtellina, Sondrio

Donation Fedital
1990

The Valtellina Valley is full of castles and strongholds because in the past it was the gateway between Northern Italy and the rest of Europe. Among these, the Castle de Piro al Grumello, more commonly known as Grumello Castle, deserves special attention. Named for the rocky outcrop, or *grumo*, on which it was built, it is a fascinating and evocative place whose ruins evoke a turbulent past. The Castle was built between the end of the thirteenth century and the beginning of the fourteenth by the Ghibelline Corrado de Piro, whose family had moved to the Valtellina following the struggles between Milan and Como. Around the middle of the fourteenth century, the de Piro family suffered a rapid decline, causing them to sell the Castle to their rivals, the Capitanei. The structure was finally destroyed in 1526 by the Grigioni, as was the fate of many other fortifications in the Valley. Grumello Castle is a rare example of a "twin" castle, composed of two bodies, one military and one residential, surrounded by walls. The military structure, to the east, was designed for defence and as a lookout point, as can be seen from the imposing square tower and the foundations of a second tower. The residential destination of the second building is confirmed by the more gently roughed-out stones and the traces of a fireplace in one of the rooms. Donated to FAI by Fedital in 1990, the Castle was restored and opened to the public in 2001.

Palazzina Appiani

Milano

Concession by
the Municipality of Milan
2015

Palazzina Appiani is a loggia with monumental classical forms born as Napoleon's royal tribune, overlooking the Milan Civic Arena where a part of the history of the last two hundred years of the city took place: from political events to cultural events, from parties to concerts, to city gatherings, and in particular some major events that have marked the history of sport in Italy. Inside, the great Hall of Honour is decorated with marble, crystal and a long frieze depicting a scene of procession, the work of Angelo Monticelli (1778–1837), a painter and figurist trained in the workshop of Andrea Appiani. Palazzina Appiani has become a FAI Property thanks to an agreement with the Municipality of Milan aimed at enhancing the place by ensuring its regular opening to the public, management and maintenance.

Cappella del Simonino

Trento

Bequest
Marina Larcher Fogazzaro
2018

The Cappella del Simonino is a chapel inside Palazzo Bortolazzi Larcher Fogazzaro, in the heart of the city of Trento, and was bequeathed to FAI by Marina Larcher Fogazzaro (1918–2018) in 2018. It rises near what was once the home of so-called "blessed Simonino", a child murdered in 1475. The inscription painted on the facade reads: "In this house was born Blessed Simon, whose body rests in the Church of San Peter and in the year of Our Lord 1475 here he was abducted". The statue of the child raising his banner presides over the portal of access to the hall, surmounted by a small bell, while another representation of Simonino can be seen in the fresco that occupies the upper part of the facade. At the time of the donation the fresco turned out to be in a poor state of conservation and was promptly restored by FAI.

Antica barberia Giacalone

Genova

Purchased from the Giacalone Heirs thanks to a public subscription
1992

Located in Vico dei Caprettari, a characteristic *caruggio*, or narrow lane, in the historical centre of Genoa, this little barber's shop is one of the oldest street shops in the city. Barely 10 square metres large, the shop was originally opened by Mr Giacalone, a barber, in 1882. A few decades later, in 1922, his son Italo redecorated the interior in the then popular deco style.
Giacalone the younger owned the shop from 1922 until 1992, the year of his death. That same year, the shop was purchased by the Genoa Delegation of FAI. Having restored the shop and re-opened it to the public, FAI has entrusted it to another celebrated Genoese barber, who plies his trade there on a daily basis.
The shop retains an evocative period atmosphere, thanks to the original furnishings, from the classic barber's armchairs to the Art Nouveau lamps, and especially to the decoration, characterised by a play of mirrors and coloured glass panes on the walls and the ceiling.

Torre di Punta Pagana

Rapallo, Genova

Donation
De Grossi Family
1981

The Torre di Punta Pagana is located a few minutes from the centre of Rapallo, on a promontory covered with pine trees. Built in the second half of the sixteenth century, it bears witness to a time when the Ligurian coasts were often subject to raids by corsair ships. The tragic pirate assault carried out in Rapallo by the Turkish admiral Dragut on 4 July 1549 prompted the inhabitants of the hamlet of San Michele to ask that the village be made more secure and and equipped with a watch tower.
In 1981 the structure was donated to FAI, which decided to restore it, also ensuring the survival of the surrounding tree species.
The conservative restoration works have restored the roof of the "bombard chamber", rediscovered the original brick floor and preserved the exterior plasterwork, dating back to the seventeenth century.
Today, Torre di Punta Pagana is one of the few Saracen towers in Liguria not incorporated into dwellings or debased by improper uses.

Teatrino di Vetriano

Pescaglia, Lucca

Donation Anna Biagioni and concession by the Municipality of Pescaglia 1997

The tiny town of Vetriano, in the municipality of Pescaglia, among the rolling Tuscan hills of Garfagnana, near Lucca, deserved an entry in the *Guinness Book of World Records* in 1997 for its theatre, considered the smallest historical public theatre in the world. The story of this little gem began in 1890 when Virgilio Biagini, an engineer, donated his barn to his fellow villagers, on the condition that they form an association to transform it into a theatre. Thanks to considerable financial commitment (each of the 22 members contributed a one-time payment of 2 Lira and an additional 50 cents a month) and the work carried out by the members themselves, the little hamlet of Vetriano managed to create its little "jewel box". In 1891, the first performances were held, including plays and musical comedies, often written and recited by residents of the village. A mere 71 square metres, the theatre featured two balconies. The stage was framed by neo-classical decorations in tempera and fresco technique. The small trapezoidal pit had no seats, so spectators brought their favourite chairs from home. Unfortunately, during the sixties, a decay period started. Thanks to the 1997 donation and to the Foundation's restoration project, in 2002 the little theatre has resumed its activity, even collaborating with the Teatro alla Scala Academy.

Giardino Pantesco Donnafugata

Isola di Pantelleria, Trapani

Donation Cantine Donnafugata
2008

The oldest representation of a garden is that engraved on a Sumerian tablet dating from 3000 BC and depicting a fruit tree surrounded by a wall. This is the first testament to the concept that would then develop over the centuries into the idea of the garden: a closed space in which trees are allowed to grow. The Giardino Pantesco – which plays host to an extraordinary, ancient "Portugal" (sweet) orange tree – takes its cue from the longstanding tradition of the "walled garden": dating back to the dawn of the culture of the warm, arid countries of the southern Mediterranean, these circular-plan structures – which house, behind a door, a single citrus tree – represent an ingenious, self-sufficient agronomic system with the capacity to defend the tree against the two main threats to its survival: wind and drought. By making the most of the porosity of the stone and the temperature shifts between night and day to capture the water directly from the atmosphere, alongside channels made from stone and rammed earth that collect the rain, the walled garden is able to meet the need for water even in the absence of irrigation. The Giardino Pantesco, generously donated to FAI by Donnafugata, a long-established Sicilian winery, is one of the few remaining, well-preserved examples, and has now been completely restored.

Batteria Militare Talmone

Palau, Sassari

Concession by the Autonomous Region of Sardinia
2002

Camouflaged in the thick Mediterranean maquis of the northern coast, for two hundred years the Talmone Gun Battery has presided over the tract of sea that separates the island of Spargi from Sardinia. The Talmone Gun Battery lets us in on the daily life of soldiers: the never-ending hours spent scrutinizing the sea from the watchtower, the dormitories, the tracking station, the implacable solitude.

In 1947, shortly after the end of the Second World War, the Paris Peace Treaties required Italy to cease using all of its coastal military facilities: the Gun Battery was, then, abandoned to the ravages of time until, in 2002, the Autonomous Region of Sardinia entrusted the Property to FAI on a concessionary basis, and it immediately underwent a painstaking process of conservative restoration. Thanks to the support of the municipality of Palau, the Talmone Gun Battery is now open to the public.

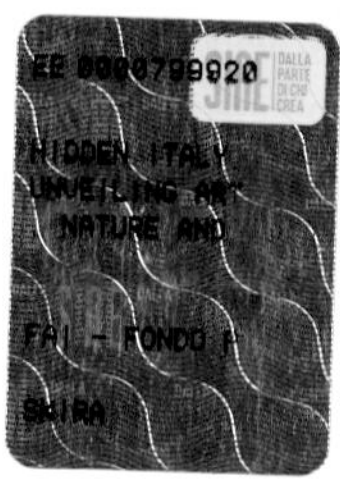

Edited by
FAI – Fondo Ambiente Italiano ETS
www.fondoambiente.it

Translations
Traduzioni Liquide - Gordon Fisher

Skira editore

Design
Marcello Francone

Editorial coordination
Marcello Francone

Copy editing
Arianna Ghilardotti

Layout
Sara Marcon

First published in Italy in 2024 by
Skira editore S.p.A.
via Agnello 18
20121 Milano
Italy
www.skira.net

Printed and bound in Italy. First edition

ISBN: 978-88-572-4260-6

Distributed in USA, Canada, Central & South America by ARTBOOK | D.A.P. 75 Broad Street, Suite 630, New York, NY 10004, USA.
Distributed elsewhere in the world by Thames and Hudson Ltd. 181A High Holborn, London WC1V 7QX, United Kingdom.

MIX
Paper | Supporting responsible forestry
FSC www.fsc.org
FSC® C013389

- Giuseppe Taibi 2021 © FAI – Fondo per l'Ambiente Italiano: cover, p. 297
- FAI – Fondo per l'Ambiente Italiano: pp. 3, 67 (top), 88–89, 133, 147, 157 (top), 186, 245 (bottom left), 268, 269 (bottom), 292, 314 (top), 315 (bottom), 317 (top), 318
- Photo Hamilton 2008 © FAI – Fondo per l'Ambiente Italiano: p. 319 (top)
- Irene Grassi © FAI – Fondo per l'Ambiente Italiano: p. 319 (bottom)
- Marco Mazzoleni © FAI – Fondo per l'Ambiente Italiano: p. 314 (bottom)
- Paolo Ioudioux © FAI – Fondo per l'Ambiente Italiano: p. 315 (top)
- Emanuele Simonaro – Parco della Valle dei Templi 2018 © FAI – Fondo per l'Ambiente Italiano: pp. 300–301
- Antonietta Abissi © FAI – Fondo per l'Ambiente Italiano: p. 302
- Andrea Mariniello © FAI – Fondo per l'Ambiente Italiano: pp. 305, 308 (top), 311 (bottom)
- Fabio Sigismondi © FAI – Fondo per l'Ambiente Italiano: p. 313 (top)
- Francesca Fossati © FAI – Fondo per l'Ambiente Italiano: p. 313 (bottom)
- Manuela Meloni © FAI – Fondo per l'Ambiente Italiano: pp. 308 (bottom), 309
- Anna Comi © FAI – Fondo per l'Ambiente Italiano: p. 317 (bottom)
- Studio Larus 2019 © FAI – Fondo per l'Ambiente Italiano: p. 293
- Gianpiero Capecchi 2016 © FAI – Fondo per l'Ambiente Italiano: pp. 294, 295
- Francesco Ammendola – Ufficio Stampa Presidenza della Repubblica: p. 245 (bottom right)
- Martina Vanzo © FAI – Fondo per l'Ambiente Italiano: pp. 4, 5, 141, 148, 154–155, 156, 157 (bottom), 172, 177 (bottom), 187, 316 (bottom)
- Tommaso Prugnola 2020 © FAI – Fondo per l'Ambiente Italiano: pp. 144–145
- Luca Chiaudano 2022 © FAI – Fondo per l'Ambiente Italiano: pp. 159, 160–161, 162–163, 164, 165
- Mauro Ranzani © FAI – Fondo per l'Ambiente Italiano: pp. 167, 170, 171, 173, 175 (top), 177 (top)
- Maurizio Bianchi © FAI – Fondo per l'Ambiente Italiano: p. 175 (bottom)
- Alessandro Torrenti 2012 © FAI – Fondo per l'Ambiente Italiano: p. 174
- Roberto Morelli 2020 © FAI – Fondo per l'Ambiente Italiano: p. 15
- Dario Fusaro © FAI – Fondo per l'Ambiente Italiano: pp. 18–19, 20–21, 37, 39, 239, 242, 243, 245 (top right)
- Maurizio Sbrozzi © FAI – Fondo per l'Ambiente Italiano: pp. 245 (top left), 278 (top)
- Andrea Straccini © FAI – Fondo per l'Ambiente Italiano: p. 244
- Giorgio Majno © FAI – Fondo per l'Ambiente Italiano: pp. 22, 51, 60 (bottom), 61, 63, 70, 71, 79, 90, 92, 93 (bottom), 100 (top), 110, 112, 113, 114–115, 117, 118, 176
- Lucia Cattoni © FAI – Fondo per l'Ambiente Italiano: p. 23
- Stefano Casiraghi © FAI – Fondo per l'Ambiente Italiano: pp. 24, 25, 126, 128 (top), 129, 130 (bottom)
- Franco Bello 2015 © FAI – Fondo per l'Ambiente Italiano: p. 27
- Marcello Francone: pp. 30–31, 73, 82 (top)
- Maria Burro © FAI – Fondo per l'Ambiente Italiano: pp. 32, 40
- Morelli – Mesturini 2022 © FAI – Fondo per l'Ambiente Italiano: pp. 34 (top), 35
- Mauro Ranzani © FAI – Fondo per l'Ambiente Italiano: p. 36
- Auda & Coudayre © FAI – Fondo per l'Ambiente Italiano: p. 38
- Paolo Robino 2015 © FAI – Fondo per l'Ambiente Italiano: p. 41
- Photo arenaimmagini.it © FAI – Fondo per l'Ambiente Italiano: pp. 43, 47, 48, 49, 78, 93 (top), 95, 98–99, 101, 105, 108–109, 111, 119 (bottom), 123, 127 (top), 135, 136, 137, 138, 139, 189, 193, 194, 195, 273, 276–277, 278 (bottom), 279 (top), 286
- Filippo Poli © FAI – Fondo per l'Ambiente Italiano: p. 287
- Antonio Leo © FAI – Fondo per l'Ambiente Italiano: pp. 288 (top), 289
- Francesco Casalenuovo 2016: p. 291
- Luca Acito © FAI – Fondo per l'Ambiente Italiano: p. 279 (bottom)
- Loretta Martella © FAI – Fondo per l'Ambiente Italiano: pp. 281, 288 (bottom)
- Antonio Leo – Fabio D'Agostino © FAI – Fondo per l'Ambiente Italiano: pp. 284–285
- Foto Archivio Comune di Morazzone: p. 44
- Gabriele Basilico © FAI – Fondo per l'Ambiente Italiano: pp. 46, 59, 119 (top), 127 (bottom), 316 (top)
- Barbara Verduci © FAI – Fondo per l'Ambiente Italiano: pp. 34 (bottom), 54–55, 56, 68–69, 211 (bottom), 212–213
- Lorenzo Monti © FAI – Fondo per l'Ambiente Italiano: p. 67
- Davide Marcesini © FAI – Fondo per l'Ambiente Italiano: pp. 215, 218–219, 220, 221, 223, 226, 228 (bottom), 229 (top)
- Giuseppe Lo Pilato © FAI – Fondo per l'Ambiente Italiano: p. 303
- Fabrizio Giordano © FAI – Fondo per l'Ambiente Italiano: p. 229 (bottom)
- Lucio Lazzara © FAI – Fondo per l'Ambiente Italiano: pp. 231, 234, 235, 236–237, 247, 253 (top), 263, 310
- Manuel Chiesa © FAI – Fondo per l'Ambiente Italiano: p. 311 (top)
- Roberto Berti 2012 © FAI – Fondo per l'Ambiente Italiano: p. 248
- Andrea Angelucci 2012 © FAI – Fondo per l'Ambiente Italiano: pp. 250 (top), 251, 252
- Foto Umbria–Foto Andrea Cittadini 2010 © FAI – Fondo per l'Ambiente Italiano: p. 253 (bottom)
- Massimo Siragusa © FAI – Fondo per l'Ambiente Italiano: pp. 255, 258
- Tommaso Bonaventura: pp. 259, 261 (top)
- Paolo Barcucci © FAI – Fondo per l'Ambiente Italiano: p. 261 (bottom)
- Patrizia Bonanzinga: pp. 260, 262
- Mimmo Jodice © FAI – Fondo per l'Ambiente Italiano: pp. 265, 266, 269 (top), 270
- Antonella De Angelis © FAI – Fondo per l'Ambiente Italiano: p. 271
- Eleonora Dottorini 2020 © FAI – Fondo per l'Ambiente Italiano: p. 250 (bottom)
- Matteo Cupella © FAI – Fondo per l'Ambiente Italiano: pp. 227, 228 (top)
- Marianne Majerus Garden Images: p. 57
- Angelisa Balzani © FAI – Fondo per l'Ambiente Italiano: p. 58
- Mario Govino © FAI – Fondo per l'Ambiente Italiano: p. 60 (top)
- Valentina Pasolini © FAI – Fondo per l'Ambiente Italiano: pp. 66, 121
- Photo www.tenderinifotografia.it 2018 © FAI – Fondo per l'Ambiente Italiano: pp. 76–77
- Photo Michele Alberto Sereni – Magonza 2020 © FAI – Fondo per l'Ambiente Italiano: pp. 80 (bottom), 81 (bottom), 82 (bottom)
- Tommaso Gesuato 2014 © FAI – Fondo per l'Ambiente Italiano: p. 33
- Giorgio Colombo: p. 80 (top), 81 (in alto), 83
- Alessio Mesiano © FAI – Fondo per l'Ambiente Italiano: cover, p. 85
- Carolina Prieto 2015 © FAI – Fondo per l'Ambiente Italiano: p. 91 (top)
- Rudi Metselaar 2016 © FAI – Fondo per l'Ambiente Italiano: p. 91 (bottom)
- Chiara Colombo 2018 © FAI – Fondo per l'Ambiente Italiano: p. 100 (bottom)
- Susy Mezzanotte 2015 © FAI – Fondo per l'Ambiente Italiano: pp. 102, 103
- Massimo Ripani: pp. 116, 117
- Photo Studio Da Re: pp. 124, 128 (bottom)
- Gimmy Schiavi © FAI – Fondo per l'Ambiente Italiano: p. 130 (top)
- Photo G. Buttazzoni-O. Kolici © FAI – Fondo per l'Ambiente Italiano: p. 131
- Vivi Papi: pp. 146, 149
- Maurizio Vento © FAI – Fondo per l'Ambiente Italiano: p. 151
- Mariangela Peci 2021 © FAI – Fondo per l'Ambiente Italiano: p. 179
- Associazione Archivio Storico Olivetti, Ivrea – Photo Giacomelli: p. 180
- Photo ORC Chemollo: pp. 182, 183
- Marco Introini: p. 184
- Luca Carli: p. 185
- Massimo Ciampi: p. 192
- Matteo Girola © FAI – Fondo per l'Ambiente Italiano: p. 197
- Luca Tamagnini Photoatlante: pp. 200–201
- Dino Zanolin 2016 © FAI – Fondo per l'Ambiente Italiano: pp. 202–203, 205
- Luigino Visconti, Genova 2004 © FAI – Fondo per l'Ambiente Italiano: pp. 207, 210, 211 (top)
- Marco Ligabue e Matteo Girola 2017 © FAI – Fondo per l'Ambiente Italiano: p. 204 (top)
- Santi Caleca © FAI – Fondo per l'Ambiente Italiano: p. 204 (bottom)